Table of Contents

Introduction 2

Abuelita 5
by Kathleen Simpson

A Letter from the President 11
by Tekla White

Girl Missionary 17
by Kathleen Simpson

First Day of School 23
by Kathleen Simpson

V-Mail and Cardboard Shoes 28
by Kathleen Simpson

Journey to America—1848 36
by Tekla White

Freedom Berries 42
by Tekla White

Let's Celebrate 49
by Tekla White

The Yellow Stars 55
by Jill Norris

Nancy Lopez and Family 61
by Kathleen Simpson

Laurence Yep 67
by Tekla White

My Great-Grandmother Bonnie 73
by Delana Heidrich

Dancing to the Drum 79
by Delana Heidrich

Corine Bunn & Growing-up Years 85
by Tekla White

Melting Pot 92
by Delana Heidrich

Jesse Owens 98
by Tekla White

Cheng Wan's Visitor 104
by Delana Heidrich

Indiana Sundays 111
by Delana Heidrich

Maria Tallchief 117
by Kathleen Simpson

Helen Keller 123
by Delana Heidrich

We Shall Overcome 129
by Delana Heidrich

Freedom Celebration 135
by Kathleen Simpson

Answer Key 139

About the Stories

Through biographies and realistic fiction, students will learn about people, events, and ideas that represent the grand diversity of the people of North America.

While providing reading practice, the 22 stories in *Read and Understand, Celebrating Diversity, Grades 4–6* present ideas and information that address diversity objectives in current standards outlined by the National Council for the Social Studies.

The stories in this book progress from fourth- to seventh-grade reading levels. When dealing with biographies and social studies content, certain specific vocabulary is necessary. For this reason, the readability of some of the stories in this book may be at a higher level than students can read independently.

How to Use the Stories

We suggest that you use the stories in this book for shared and guided reading experiences. Prior to reading, be sure to introduce any vocabulary that students may find difficult to decode or understand. A list of suggested words to teach is given on pages 3 and 4.

The Skills Pages

Each story is followed by up to four pages of activities covering specific reading skills:

- comprehension
- vocabulary
- making connections to students' own lives—comparison, evaluation, feelings
- making connections to the curriculum—mathematics, geography, written language, etc.

The content of the stories in *Read and Understand, Celebrating Diversity, Grades 4–6* requires that specific vocabulary be used. This vocabulary is often at a higher level than might be expected for the grade level. We suggest, therefore, that you introduce these words before presenting the story. It is also advisable to read the story in advance to pinpoint additional words that your students may not know.

Abuelita 5
Abuelita, Mexico, Spanish, oleander, *sí*, *Creo que sí*, *gracias*

A Letter from the President 11
Japanese, reparation, serious injustices, Tule Lake, interned, confined, New Jersey, valuable, college

Girl Missionary 17
exasperated, Christine, Tamara, missionary, dramatic, necessarily, considered, license, medical clinic, weird, religious, hesitated, selfishly, nervous, relieved, compete

First Day of School 23
haiku, Japanese, syllables, usually, image

V-Mail and Cardboard Shoes 28
humongous, wedged, flurries, ordinary, imitation, Official Business, pored, miniature, comedians, dominoes, lightweight, connection, overseas, static, ration coupons

Journey to America—1848 36
O'Brien, Bridget, Finney, Boston, Ireland, passengers, examined, Nicholas, boarding house, Beckett House

Freedom Berries 42
Jebediah, Quaker, slave-catcher, hitched, compartment, Rebecca, rearranged, reins

Let's Celebrate 49
pan de muertos, El día de los muertos, Elena, rehearsals, acquainted, altar, skeletons, ancestors, cemetery, marigolds, arrange

The Yellow Stars 55
Nazi, antisemitism, genocidal, regime, Aryan, eliminate, suspended, synagogues, curfews, vandalized, ghettos

Nancy Lopez and Family 61
bored, regularly, Marina, Domingo, pointers, Cahoon Park, courses, challenging, expensive, compete, accomplishment, displayed, amateur tournament, barriers, disappointed, determined, attorney, required, Roswell, honorary, championship, racial prejudice, sponsor, Albuquerque, professional

Laurence Yep 67
San Francisco, imaginary, education, science fiction, Chinatown district, customs, relatives, adjust, produced, Catholic school, advanced, chemistry, college, journalism, Marquette University, fiction, Selchey Kids, Joanne Ryder, publisher

My Great-Grandmother Bonnie 73
ten and three-quarters, terrifically, humidity, enormous, Garrett Library, privy, icebox, gargle, vinegar, herbal tea

Dancing to the Drum 79
powwow, Native American celebration, reservations, celebrate, honor, costumes, rawhide, arena, traditional, heritage, competition, unusual, rhythms, ability, distinct symbols, history, culture

Corine Bunn & Growing-up Years 85
Corine Bunn, ninetieth, mayor, Oakland, Hillary Rodham Clinton, community, crocheted, volunteered, Baptist, achievements, senior citizens, elderly, Locust Bayou, Arkansas, midwife, Sears catalog, molasses, syrup

Melting Pot 92
perfectly, history, European, Philippines, varied, demonstrate, unique, represented, heritages, admire, culture, enthusiasm, cafeteria, responded, adopted, entirely, biological, adoptive, ancestors, nutcracker, Jamaica, contributions, addition

Jesse Owens 98
Jesse Cleveland Owens, Danville, technical, national, graduated, university, scholarship, sophomore, Michigan, hurdles, Berlin, Germany, Olympics, government, Adolph Hitler, athletes, inferior, congratulated, stadium, befriended, gigantic, discrimination, professional, exhibitions, scheduled, legendary, Harlem Globetrotters, disk jockey, physically, recognized, achievements

Cheng Wan's Visitor 104
Cheng Wan, Montana, business, diary, introduced, conducted, almond, replaced, impressed, curiously, gilded, symbols, *dia fau*, intricate, oriental, famine, peasant rebellions, immigrants, Portsmouth Square, economy, tragedy, earthquake, repopulate, Kearney and Stockton Streets, residents, marveled, gorgeous, disappointed, fortune cookie, herbal teas, impression

Indiana Sundays 111
precisely, disorderly, devour, wheelbarrows, complaints, domain, assured, eventually, volleyball, clamored, mosquito, retired, collapsing, ethics, conscience, resolved, issues, cellar, elders, cramped, massive, rickety, self-respecting, recreation, debate, attractions, frequently, surrendered, brood, reluctant

Maria Tallchief 117
ballerina, inherited, bearing, grace, Osage, reservation, prominent, imposing, career, Irish, Scottish, ambition, concert pianist, Bronislava Nijinska, Russia, demanding, encouragement, professional ballet company, concerned, Ballet Russe de Monte Carlo, George Balanchine, choreographer, original, prima ballerina, enchanting, electrifying, Chicago Lyric Opera Ballet, Hamburg Ballet, Oklahoma

Helen Keller 123
Tuscumbia, Alabama, Lioness, Europe, concerns, communicating, frustrated, dashed, fragile, objects, temper tantrums, tutor, accomplishments, mastered, French, German, Greek, Latin, toboggan, translated, graduation, Massachusetts Commission for the Blind, prime ministers, independence, justice, audiences, dignity, assistant, organizations, disadvantaged, companion, determination

We Shall Overcome 129
American Civil War, constitutional amendments, injustices, abolished, citizens, discrimination, shameful, Supreme Court, invalidated, legally barred, establishments, mourned, assuring, endure, pastor, mistreatment, arrested, National Association for the Advancement of Colored People, boycott, Montgomery, integrated, massive movement, civil rights, Southern Christian Leadership Conference, oppose, uniting, eloquent, remarkable, insistence, organized, segregation, expressed, harmony, thunderous, applause, quoted

Freedom Celebration 135
Civil War, Abraham Lincoln, Emancipation Proclamation, Galveston, absolute, equality, connection, idleness, employer, advised, military, assure, Juneteenth, barbecue, racial prejudice

Abuelita

David knew his grandmother missed Mexico. She walked with him on the beach and talked about the mountains there and the green hills that spread out like a wrinkled blanket. She talked about the friends she had left behind. David rattled the seashells in his pockets and listened.

She let the waves swirl around her feet as she stared out across the gulf toward Mexico. Their neighbor's dog, which had followed them on their walk, licked her ankle and whined.

"Old Dog," Abuelita said in Spanish, "are you hungry? Your master should feed you." She shook her head.

David's grandmother didn't trust their neighbor, Mrs. Bass. She didn't trust anyone who did not speak Spanish. David thought that if his grandmother made some friends, she might be happier. "I think Mrs. Bass takes good care of the dog, Abuelita," said David.

The old woman took David's arm and said in Spanish, "Let's go home and feed this poor old dog."

They made their way down a sandy stretch of road to the house where they lived. The dog lay down on the porch in the shade of some oleander bushes. "I think he would like some meat," David said. "He looks like a dog that likes meat."

"*Sí,*" said Abuelita. She took some meat from the refrigerator and put it in a bowl in front of the dog. David and his grandmother watched him mouth the meat and whine.

"Why isn't he eating?" David asked.

Abuelita knelt in front of the dog, his head in her hand. When she felt with her fingers along his jaw, he jerked back and growled. "It's all right, Old Dog." She scratched behind his ears. "I won't hurt you again."

"What's wrong with him?" David asked.

"He has a toothache, I think," said his grandmother.

A screen door slammed at Mrs. Bass's house. In her high, old-lady voice, she called for the dog. "Gen-eral! General, where are you?"

"He's over here, Mrs. Bass," David called in English.

Mrs. Bass clumped up the steps and shyly poked her head around the bushes. "Good morning," she said.

"Good morning," said David. Abuelita nodded stiffly.

"We thought he was hungry," said David, "but he won't eat."

"I know." Mrs. Bass shook her head sadly. "Poor General. I don't know what to do. I can't get him to eat anything."

"My grandmother thinks he has a toothache," said David.

"Really?" Mrs. Bass looked at Abuelita in surprise. "A toothache? Is that all it is?"

David could tell that his grandmother was proud of having figured out the problem. Abuelita nodded again, this time with a little smile. *"Creo que sí."* I think so.

"I'll take him to the vet." Mrs. Bass looked at David with tearful eyes. "I'm so glad it's only that. He's so old, I thought…I was afraid it was something much worse." She turned to Abuelita. "Thank you. *Gracias.*"

Without looking up, Abuelita said in English, "You are welcome."

Name_____

Questions about *Abuelita*

1. Why did the dog jerk back and growl when David's grandmother felt along his jaw with her fingers?

_____

2. What is the setting of the story? How do you know?

_____

_____

3. Why doesn't David's grandmother trust Mrs. Bass?

_____

_____

4. How do you think Mrs. Bass feels about General? Support your opinion with facts from the story.

_____

_____

5. How would you describe David's grandmother?

_____

_____

6. What occurrence might lead you to believe that Abuelita will change her mind about Mrs. Bass?

_____

7. What do you think will happen next in the story?

_____

_____

Abuelita
Vocabulary

A. The underlined words below are specific and descriptive. Write other specific, descriptive words that could be used in the sentences. The first one has been done as an example.

1. Mrs. Bass <u>clumped</u> up the steps.

   <u>tramped, stomped, thudded</u>_____

2. David <u>rattled</u> the seashells in his pockets.

   _____

3. Abuelita <u>stared</u> out across the gulf.

   _____

4. The dog <u>jerked</u> back and growled.

   _____

5. David and Abuelita walked down a sandy <u>stretch</u> of road to David's house.

   _____

6. Mrs. Bass called in a <u>high</u>, old-lady voice.

   _____

7. Mrs. Bass <u>shyly</u> poked her head around the bushes.

   _____

8. Mrs. Bass looked at David with <u>tearful</u> eyes.

   _____

B. Write the Spanish words from the story to match the English words below. Use clues in the story to help you.

1. I think so _____

2. Grandmother_____

3. thank you _____

4. yes _____

Name_____

Abuelita

Making Friends

1. If you were David, what would you do to help your grandmother make friends?

_____

_____

_____

_____

2. Have you ever felt unsure about someone who seemed different, then changed your mind when you got to know that person better? Write about a time when your feelings changed after you got to know someone.

_____

_____

_____

_____

_____

_____

_____

Abuelita

Reading a Map

Study the map. Then answer the questions below.

1. Which states border the Gulf of Mexico?

   _____

2. Which state on the Gulf of Mexico is closest to Mexico?

   _____

3. Is this state north, south, east, or west of Mexico?

   _____

4. Name the three cities in which the story could have taken place.

   _____

5. A *peninsula* is a piece of land that is surrounded on three sides by water.
   Which state on the Gulf of Mexico is a peninsula?

   _____

6. Name two major rivers that empty into the Gulf of Mexico.

   _____   _____

 # A Letter from the President

Sam set his books on the table and looked for Gramps. Gramps was in charge of the house while Sam's mom and dad were at work. The patio door was open. Gramps was sitting on a garden bench. He didn't look at Sam or say hello.

"He's probably tired of waiting," Sam thought. "I'm late, but Gramps shouldn't be mad. I was working on my science project. He's always telling me to study."

Sam picked up a letter off the floor. It had President George Bush's name on it.

He took the letter to Gramps. "You got a letter from the president?" he asked.

Gramps nodded. "And twenty thousand dollars."

"How come?" Sam asked. "Is the president hiring you to write his speeches or something?"

"It's reparation for being in the camp," Gramps said. "It's a payment from the government."

"What camp? What's a reparation?" Sam didn't understand very much—just that "serious injustices" were done to Japanese Americans during World War II.

"I should have talked to you about it before. I was afraid you'd think I'd done something wrong, so I didn't say anything. Now the president says the government was wrong—not the Japanese Americans.

"The United States came into World War II after the Japanese Air Force bombed Pearl Harbor in Hawaii in 1941. The government thought Japanese Americans were dangerous and that they would try to help Japan. My family had to leave our farm. We sold some of the animals and I gave my dog to a friend at school. I couldn't keep him. We could just take what we could carry."

"Where did you go?" Sam asked.

"We were sent to Tule Lake, California. There were soldiers and barbed wire to keep us interned, or confined, inside the camp."

"How could they do that if you didn't do anything?" Sam asked.

"We had to do what the soldiers said."

"Did you have a house there?" Sam asked.

"We had one room for the whole family. There was a building for showers and a dining hall for meals. There wasn't much rice or meat. We raised some chickens. After a few weeks people started classes. My father helped make furniture for the camp. My mother sewed. Some people started a school."

"You stayed in a camp for the whole war?" Sam asked. "Just like a prisoner? No one realized the government made a mistake?"

"Some people knew it was wrong, but no one did anything about it. My brother Mike left the camp to fight in the war for the United States. He and other Japanese American soldiers were in the 442nd Division in the army. Mike didn't come home. He lost his life proving he was a good American."

"After the war, what did you do?" Sam asked.

"When we went home, someone was living on our farm. They had papers that said the land belonged to them. Farmers wouldn't hire my dad because he was Japanese. There was this company that made frozen and canned food in New Jersey. They hired people from the camps because they were good workers. We went there. The company had schools and houses. My parents worked hard and saved their money so my brother, sister, and I could go to college."

"Are you going to take a trip or buy a new car with the money?" Sam asked.

"No," Gramps said. "I'm going to put it in a fund for your college. That's the best way to spend it. During the war, we lost our freedom and all the things we had. But no one could take what we had learned away from us. That's why I want you to study. You'll have something valuable you can carry with you—something you can always use."

President of the United States of America
1600 Pennsylvania Avenue
Washington, D.C.

Mr. Samuel Uchida
100 Main Street
Hometown, California
90000

Questions about *A Letter from the President*

1. Why did Gramps receive a letter from President Bush?

_____

_____

2. What happened to many Japanese people who lived in the United States during World War II? Why?

_____

_____

3. Describe the camp where Gramps lived during World War II.

_____

_____

_____

4. How did Gramps' family lose their farm?

_____

_____

5. What does Gramps want to do with the money he received? Why?

_____

_____

Name_____

A Letter from the President
Vocabulary

Complete the crossword puzzle using the words in the Word Box.

Across

3. the system that sets and enforces rules

4. unfair actions

7. islands that became a state in 1959

8. a person who is confined or not allowed freedom

10. confined

11. money set aside for a special purpose

Down

1. fencing with pieces of sharp wire that poke out

2. important; severe

5. people from the country of Japan

6. payment for wrongs done to others

9. understood

Name_____

A Letter from the President

A Good Friend

Imagine that you are Sam's friend and he has left his dog with you. Write a letter to Sam about the dog. You can write about the places you go and what you do.

Dear Sam,

_____

_____

_____

_____

_____

_____

_____

_____

_____

Your friend,

_____

(name)

Name_____

A Letter from the President
A History Lesson

Read the following information about laws and court rulings that affected the way Japanese Americans lived.

Fill in the spaces using words from the Word Box. Use clues in the sentences and the story to help you decide which words to use.

Word Box				
law	illegal	citizens	internment	Hawaii
discriminated	California	immigrants	detention	

    Asian Americans contributed much to the growth of the United States. They helped build the railroads that connected the western part of the country with the East. They worked on farms and operated businesses in _____, _____, and other western states. Despite these contributions, there were earlier laws that _____ against Japanese Americans and other Asians living in the United States.

    In 1913 the Alien Land Act in California made it _____ for Asians to own land for farming or other purposes. Immigrants often recorded names of their relatives or children who were born here as the owners. That way they could have a place to farm. In 1920 it became illegal in California for Asian _____ to rent or farm land belonging to someone else.

    In 1922 courts in the U.S. ruled that people born in Japan could not become _____ of the United States.

    In 1924 a _____ was passed that banned all immigration from Asia.

    In spite of these laws and their _____ during World War II in _____ camps, Japanese Americans did not give up their dreams for equal rights. They have worked and studied to become scientists, lawyers, doctors, business people, and successful farmers.

"I can't just *not* go," Christine said, exasperated. Tamara was not even trying to understand. "My *parents* are going!"

Sunlight spattered the cool grass. Tamara's fingers pushed through it into the dirt. "Actually," she said, "you could. You could stay with us. My parents would take care of you, if you didn't want to go. I know they would."

"I want to go. It's hard to leave some people, like you. And it's going to be hard to do without the things that I'm used to, but I want to go." Christine looked away. She didn't want to hurt Tamara's feelings, but she would never, not in a million years, stay here for five years when her brother and her missionary parents were going to Africa.

A deep sigh came from Tamara. Christine didn't look at her. Sometimes her friend could be pretty dramatic. Drama wasn't necessarily a bad thing, but Tamara sometimes used it just to get people to do what she wanted. This time, what she wanted was not even to be considered. "I'm sorry," Christine told her. "I'll write to you and I'll e-mail you, and I'll come back to visit once a year. We can still be friends."

"Oh, *right*," responded Tamara. "You'll be starting college when you get back. You'll be a different person. We both will be." She yanked up a handful of grass and threw it. "I don't understand why you want to go, anyway. You won't have any friends, and you can't go to a movie or the mall. You probably won't even have a driver's license when you come back! I'll be driving all over the place, dating boys, and who will you be?"

Christine sighed. Tamara made things seem pretty bleak. It was a good question: who *would* she be? Would she fit in when she came back? The answer to that one was obvious. She had never fit in with the kids Tamara knew. She pushed at her glasses with one finger.

"Look," Christine said, finally making eye contact with her friend, "we're not the same *now*. You go to public school and know lots of kids. I go to school at home and have just a few close friends. You go to the movies on Sunday afternoon. I go to church and then Sunday school. I know you believe in God, but I don't think you think about that as much as I do. But even though we're really different, we're still friends.

"It's true that if I help my parents run a medical clinic in Africa for the next five years, I'm not going to do the same kinds of things you'll be doing. But I wouldn't anyway, even if we stayed here. We don't have to be doing the same things to be friends, do we?"

For a few seconds, the girls' eyes locked. Christine looked for something in Tamara's face that would tell her it would be okay. She needed to know that her best friend wouldn't stare at her five years from now, and think, "How could I ever have been friends with this weird religious kid?" She needed to know that Tamara knew they were different and still liked her.

"Are you scared?" whispered Tamara.

"You mean, like, scared of lions and snakes and stuff?"

"No. Well, yeah, that too." Tamara hesitated. "But I also mean like, scared of being in a place where everything is different, and the food is weird and all. And what about boys? I mean, I'm not allowed to go out on dates anyway, but in a few years…. You're going to be in this clinic out in the middle of nowhere. Will there be boys there?"

"Not many, I think." It *was* a little scary. She didn't worry about snakes and lions too much, and her parents had assured her they would cook foods that the family was used to eating. But she'd felt shy about bringing up the question of boys. "I don't know what will happen." She laughed. "But I get nervous when I think about boys, anyway—even the boys here at home!"

Tamara laughed with her. "Me too, I guess!" They were silent for a moment before Tamara asked again, this time with a little groan, "But why do you *want* to go, Christine?"

What Christine heard in her friend's question was, "Why do you want to leave *me*?" Selfishly, she was relieved to hear it. She was glad that Tamara felt sad about her going. But she didn't say that to her friend. "My parents and my brother are going," she said gently. "I want to be where they are." There was also something else. She wasn't sure Tamara would understand, but she tried. "And I want to do some good. I think this is what God wants me to do."

"Oh, fine," Tamara teased. "Bring God into it! How can I compete with that?"

Christine shrugged. "You don't compete with God, Tamara. You don't have to compete with anybody. You're my best friend."

Tamara pulled up another handful of grass and threw it at her. "I still don't get it," she said. "But you're my best friend too."

Questions about *Girl Missionary*

1. What was Christine's family planning to do in Africa?

_____

_____

2. Why did Christine want to go?

_____

_____

3. What was Christine afraid might happen upon her return in five years?

_____

_____

4. What did Christine need to know from Tamara?

_____

_____

5. When a writer tells about only one character's thoughts and feelings, we say the story is written from that character's **point of view**. From which character's point of view is this story told? How do you know? Give examples.

_____

_____

_____

6. Why do you think the story is entitled *Girl Missionary*?

_____

_____

Girl Missionary
Vocabulary

Use these words and phrase from the story to complete the sentences below.

obvious	eye contact	selfishly	assured	bleak
considered	necessarily	dramatic	missionary	exasperated

1. Ray thought about three long months without his friend, Andy, to play with. Suddenly summer vacation seemed pretty _____.

2. "How could I have missed something so _____?" Maria wondered. Her mistake seemed to jump off the page at her.

3. Will _____ decided not to share his lemonade.

4. I kept trying to make _____ with Melanie, but she wouldn't look at me.

5. Each year my church sends a _____ to South America. This person's job is to teach young mothers about good nutrition for their children.

6. Those boys do look a lot alike, but that doesn't _____ mean they are twins. They might be, or they might not.

7. "You need to know this," Ms. Menendez _____ her students. "It *will* be on the test."

8. Sue made a _____ exit, flinging her hair over her shoulder and slamming the door.

9. I _____ everything you said. But after thinking about it, I still think Juanita is right.

10. After baby-sitting his two-year-old brother for an hour, Blake felt completely

    _____. The little boy had really gotten on his nerves.

Girl Missionary
Write a Story

Choose one of the topics below. On another sheet of paper, write a story about it.

There were two sides to Christine: she was Tamara's friend and she was a member of a missionary family. Her role as a missionary complicated her friendship with Tamara. Write a story, true or make-believe, about a person who has more than one role.

Have you ever felt that you didn't fit in? Why did you feel that way? Do you think you were really very different when that happened? Tell what happened and explain how you felt.

Think about what might happen in five years when Christine comes back from Africa. Will she and Tamara still be best friends? Will the two girls be more different than ever? Will that matter? Write a story about Christine's return.

       Celebrating Diversity • EMC 798

Name_____

Girl Missionary
Understanding Time Lines

A **time line** helps you understand how events are related in time. The time line below shows how Christine will get ready for her journey. Look it over carefully and then answer the questions.

September 1

Christine begins sorting through her things, deciding what to take and what to leave behind.

September 7

Christine's family has a yard sale, selling many things they can't take along.

September 17

Christine sends out cards to her friends, giving them her e-mail address.

September 24

The girls have Tamara's mother take several photos of them together. They get the photos developed at a one-hour photo shop. Each girl picks some to keep.

September 29

The family donates their furniture and cars to their church.

September 30

The girls have a farewell camp-out in Tamara's backyard. They exchange gifts. (Both girls give stationery for writing letters.)

October 1

Someone from Christine's church drives the family to the airport.

1. What time period does this time line show?

_____

2. How much time passes between the camp-out and Christine's departure?

_____

3. How many days does Christine have to sort through her things before the yard sale?

_____

The **haiku** is an ancient form of Japanese poetry. It usually does not rhyme. The first line has five syllables. The second line has seven syllables. The third line has five again, for a total of seventeen syllables. Because it is so short, the haiku sets a mood by describing only important details. The reader fills in the rest of the image.

The following poem is really two haiku verses. Read it with a partner. One person should read the verse on the left. The other person should read the verse on the right.

First-day chatter floats
in the air. Wait—who is this
stranger, looking lost?

Strange people! Strange sounds!
Wait—who is this? Ah, a smile!
That, I understand.

Questions about *First Day of School*

1. Is this poem set in a quiet place or a noisy one? How do you know?

_____

2. What else can you tell about the setting of *First Day of School*?

_____

_____

3. How many main characters are in the poem?

_____

4. As you read the verse on the left, what can you tell about this character?

_____

_____

5. In the verse on the right, how did the character feel at the beginning of the verse? What clues help you know?

_____

_____

6. What happened to change the way the character on the right felt?

_____

7. Why might that character think the people and the sounds were "strange"?

_____

_____

First Day of School
Synonyms

Synonyms are words with similar meanings. Write a synonym for the underlined word in each sentence. Then write a sentence using the synonym. Use the words below to help you.

beamed	peculiar	drifts

1. A single puff of cloud <u>floats</u> overhead. _____

_____

_____

2. Marco found himself surrounded by <u>strange</u> creatures. _____

_____

_____

3. The tall boy looked at Jenny and <u>smiled</u>. _____

_____

_____

Descriptive Words

Replace each underlined word with at least three other descriptive words. The words do <u>not</u> need to mean the same as the underlined word.

1. First-day <u>chatter</u> floats in the air.

_____

2. Who is this stranger, looking <u>lost</u>?

_____

3. Ah, a <u>smile</u>! That, I understand.

_____

First Day of School
A Scary Situation

One character in the *First Day of School* felt nervous and uneasy about the new situation at school. She may have been frightened that she wouldn't know what to do or how to speak to the strangers there.

Have you ever been in a new situation when you felt unsure of yourself and a little scared because everything was new and different? Tell about it. What happened to make you feel more "at home"?

_____

_____

_____

_____

_____

_____

_____

_____

_____

_____

First Day of School

Greetings Here and There

A. In *First Day of School,* one character greets the other with a smile. Below are greetings from around the world. Some sound much like English. Others are quite different.

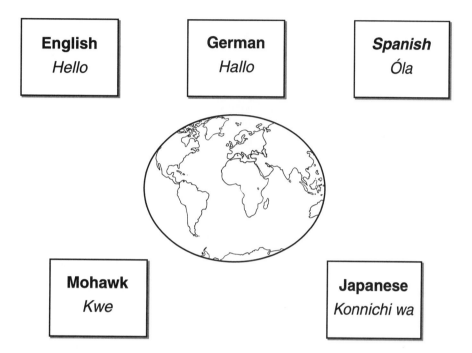

| English | German | *Spanish* |
| Hello | Hallo | Óla |

| Mohawk | Japanese |
| Kwe | Konnichi wa |

What other greetings do you know?

_____

B. Complete the sentences below using the correct form of *hello.*

1. The Mohawk people say, "_____."

2. In Germany, the word for *hello* is _____.

3. Japanese people say, " _____"

4. The English word for *hello* is _____.

5. In Mexico they say, "_____"

"Watch where you step up there!" Grandpa called. "There's a pull string to turn on the light."

Daniel didn't like the dark, dusty attic. "I don't see what this place has to do with Clark's humongous feet," he grumbled.

I turned on the light. "They're not humongous," I said, but they were. I had the biggest feet in the sixth grade.

"Do you see it?" called Grandpa. "It should be wedged between some boards on the back wall."

I saw it. When I touched the wooden box, globs of dust floated to the ground. The box was stuck fast. "Come here," I said to Daniel. "It's stuck."

Together, we wrapped our hands around it and pulled as hard as we could. When the box suddenly scraped free, Daniel fell to the attic floor. His fall sent up low flurries of dust.

"You boys all right?" Grandpa asked when he heard the thud.

"Daniel fell, but he's not hurt." I helped my brother up. "I guess my *humongous* feet helped me keep my balance." I heard Grandpa laugh.

When we brought the box down, Grandpa led us to the kitchen table. He sat down before opening it.

"What's in it?" Daniel wanted to know.

"Cardboard shoes," said Grandpa. "Size humongous."

Cardboard shoes? I was as confused as Daniel was, and I said so.

"Well, you see, Clark," said Grandpa, "your mother told me how unhappy you were about outgrowing your favorite shoes. I remembered something I hadn't thought about in over fifty years." He took a shoe out of the box, handing it to me. "The same thing happened to me in…." He reached into the box, pulled out a crumbling brown envelope, and read, "in 1945."

The shoe in my hand looked like an ordinary shoe, but really old. It seemed pretty lightweight too. Compared to these, my new, sort of huge sneakers didn't seem so bad. "Are they really cardboard?" I asked.

Grandpa nodded. "They were called imitation leather, I think, but they're actually cardboard. In 1945 America was at war. There were an awful lot of soldiers needing shoes. The government told families here at home that they could buy only so many leather shoes each year. When a boy outgrew his leather shoes, he got shoes made of something else like canvas or cardboard. Those shoes weren't as good as leather ones, though."

He wiped some of the dust off the cardboard shoe in my hand. "I had fast-growing feet, like you. My leather shoes were pretty important to me. When my feet outgrew them, I tried to keep it from my mother. I didn't want to give them to my brother, Arthur. Arthur told Mother that my shoes were too small. I think his were probably too small too, and he wanted mine. Anyway, she gave him mine and took me to the store to buy a pair of cardboard shoes. Boy, was I mad!"

He paused, his thumbs stroking the envelope. It was smaller than a normal envelope—maybe two or three inches square. The front of it read "War & Navy Departments, V-mail Service, Official Business." He went on, "Then we got a letter from my daddy, who was stationed at an air base in Italy. He wrote about how he missed us all, and we missed him terribly. Mother pored over his letter for hours."

From the little envelope, Grandpa took a miniature letter and handed it to me. In shrunken handwriting, the letter read:

February 10, 1945

Dear Linda,
    Just a few lines to let you know I'm okay. I've been here for four weeks now and still have gotten no mail. I sure hope it catches up with me soon.
    This is the rainiest place I have ever seen. I miss our warm house, Saturday night dominoes, and Jack Benny on the radio. Most of all, I miss you and the boys. Give them each a hug for me.
    Write often. I'll get all your letters eventually, I think.
                                    Love,
                                    Ben

Turning the letter over in my hands, I asked, "Why is it so small?"

"And who's Jack Benny?" Daniel piped.

"Jack Benny," Grandpa smiled, "had a radio show. You see, we had no television or video games then. After dinner we gathered around the radio and listened to mystery plays, news reports, or comedians, like Jack Benny. On Saturday nights we all went over to somebody's house. There the adults played dominoes. We kids played outside in the dark.

"The letter is small because it's a V-letter. These were made small, so they would be lightweight. That way lots of letters could be flown across the ocean. They got home faster than regular mail. Letters were our main connection to my daddy, so they were very important."

"Didn't you have a phone?" I asked.

"It wasn't easy back then to call overseas," Grandpa answered. "It sometimes took all day to get a call through. Then, often as not, there was so much static we could barely hear each other."

Daniel got up and poured himself a glass of water. "So does this have something to do with Clark's humongous feet?" he asked. He always seemed to want to talk about my humongous feet.

"In a way," said Grandpa. "I was so mad about having to give Arthur my shoes that I took Daddy's letter and my cardboard shoes. I hid them in the attic. It was pure meanness." He shook his head slowly. "I told Mother I'd lost the shoes. Arthur got a pair of canvas shoes. Mother let me wear my leather ones to school until our ration coupons came in. After a few months my feet had grown so much I could hardly get those shoes on. How they did hurt! Mother never said a word about the letter, but I think she knew I took it."

Daniel asked, "What are ration coupons?"

"Well, you see, lots of things were hard to get during the war, because the soldiers needed so many things. Leather, tires, gasoline...all these things were rationed. That meant people couldn't buy them without ration coupons from the government. Everybody got enough coupons to buy what they really needed, but no more than that."

I couldn't help myself. I had to look under the table. I was astounded to see two normal-sized feet attached to Grandpa's legs. "What happened to your feet, Grandpa?" I asked. "They're not big now."

He looked meaningfully at me and said, "I grew into them. And you will too." Then he told me to put my foot on the edge of the table. Holding the cardboard shoe up to it, he laughed. "Would you look at that!"

Daniel's jaw dropped. "Grandpa!"

"How old were you when your feet were that big?" I asked.

Scratching his head, he mused, "Well, let's see, that was 1945, so that means I was 11 years old. A year younger than you!"

We all laughed out loud. The shoe was at least an inch longer than mine!

Questions about *V-Mail and Cardboard Shoes*

1. Where did Daniel and Clark find the box? What was in it?

_____

_____

2. When did Grandpa hide the box? Why did he do it?

_____

_____

3. Why did Grandpa want to show the shoes to Clark?

_____

_____

4. How was family life different for Grandpa's family back in 1945?

_____

_____

5. Why were many things in short supply in 1945?

_____

_____

6. How do you think Grandpa felt, as a grown-up, about having hidden the letter from his mother so long ago? What clues in the story help you to know?

_____

_____

V-Mail and Cardboard Shoes
Vocabulary

A. Read the sentences below. Then write as many synonyms as you can for the underlined words. Use the back of the paper if you need more room.

1. Daniel called Clark's feet <u>humongous.</u>

   _____   _____   _____

   _____   _____   _____

   _____   _____   _____

2. The letter was described as <u>miniature</u>.

   _____   _____   _____

   _____   _____   _____

   _____   _____   _____

B. Use these words to complete the sentences below.

    wedged   dominoes   astounded   comedian   mused

1. Robert keeps everyone laughing with his jokes. He is such a _____!

2. My brother's favorite game is _____. He likes to build things with the little blocks when we are finished playing.

3. Outside Katie's back door, there is an emergency key _____ between two bricks.

4. I expected to get an "A" on my book report. When Ms. Wu handed it to me, I was _____ to see a "C" at the top of my paper.

5. "Hmm," the teacher _____, "let me think about that question for a moment."

            Celebrating Diversity • EMC 798

Name_____

V-Mail and Cardboard Shoes

Then and Now

1. When Grandpa was a boy, his family liked to spend free time listening to the radio or playing dominoes with friends. How do you like to spend your free time?

_____

_____

_____

2. What are some other ways in which Grandpa's childhood was different from yours? How was it the same?

_____

_____

_____

3. The letter from Grandpa's father reveals a lot about what life was like for this family in the 1940s. Write a letter to your future grandchildren. Tell them what you would like them to know about the way you live now.

_____

_____

_____

_____

_____

_____

Name_____

V-Mail and Cardboard Shoes
Getting the Word Out

When Grandpa was a boy, most people communicated with each other through the written word, radio, or telephone. The words below describe ways in which communication has changed since 1945. Use the words in the Word Box to complete the crossword puzzle.

Across

4. a powerful electronic tool that stores and processes information

5. this word often refers to television signals that are carried into homes and businesses on a wire

6. a web of information that can be accessed with a computer and a phone line

8. a short form of the word *facsimile;* a machine that sends pictures of printed material over the phone line

9. a machine that receives electromagnetic signals and changes them into sound and pictures on a screen, so that you can watch your favorite show

Down

1. a type of disc that plays music, games, or computer programs

2. it orbits the earth, collecting and/or sending information

3. to send electronically

4. a kind of phone that can be used anywhere, even outside or in the car

7. electronic mail

Word Box

e-mail	computer
Internet	cellular
compact	fax
cable	transmit
television	satellite

I didn't want to let go, but Mr. O'Brien gently moved me away from Mother. "There now, Bridget," he said, "I'll be leaving you behind if you don't hurry." He picked me up and set me in the wagon next to my brother Paul.

Mother took off her shawl and wrapped it around me. "A little bit of Ireland to keep you warm when you're on the sailing ship."

"Take good care of them, Mary Finney," Mother said as the horses started out.

"Like my own," Mary replied. "I'll take them to your brother when we reach Boston."

Our bags were filled with food for the long journey. It was all Mother could spare. The potato crop had rotted. All the wheat we raised went to pay the tax collector.

Uncle James, Mother's brother, sailed to America two years ago. He wrote to tell Mother what a fine place Boston was. He sent some money with a sailor who was returning to Ireland. There wasn't enough for all of us to go to America. When Mother's friend, Mary, was leaving to join her husband in Boston, Mother decided it would be better for us there. She promised she would come later.

Paul, who was eight, two years younger than I, started to cry. I held his hand as tight as I could. "We're together," I said. "We'll help each other." Someone in the back of the wagon started to sing a song about leaving Ireland. Soon everyone was singing.

It was a long journey to the ship that would take us to America. We stopped at night to rest the horses. People slept in the wagon or under it. I made sure Paul ate very little of the food in his bag so it would last the whole voyage.

When we reached the dock, Mary told the official that we were her dear children. He looked us over and then wrote on some papers and handed them to Mary.

Sailors helped us on board and sent us to a room below the deck. We found three beds that hadn't been taken. The beds were hard boards that were stacked like the shelves in Mother's kitchen—one above the other. That first night we slept poorly, listening to the creaking ship rock on the waves.

During the long days at sea, we sang and listened to the stories the passengers told. Paul, Mary, and I took turns keeping the rats away from our food. We shared our provisions with those who had little to eat. Many people were sick during the voyage. Sometimes the sickness was caused by the boat rocking on the waves, but often people came down with the fever. Two people died.

We sailed six weeks before we reached Boston. When we left the ship, Paul and I stood on the dock, breathing the fresh air. Mary didn't feel well, but she laughed and joked while the doctors examined us so they would think she was healthy. No one who came off that ship felt well. The smells from all the people crowded together for so long made everyone ill.

Mary sent word to her husband Nicholas that we were in Boston. He came the next morning.

We rode to Uncle James's boarding house in a wagon Nicholas had borrowed. A young woman answered the door.

"We've come to see James." Nicholas said.

"I'd like to see him too," the woman answered. "He's gone without paying the rent that was due. He didn't come back yesterday evening."

Nicholas took some coins from his pockets. "Take this for what you're due. Send James's belongings to Nicholas Finney at the Beckett House. I'll be found in the rooms over the stable."

"I don't know where to look for James," Nicholas said when we were in the wagon. "He may have left the city for work. Don't worry, he'll write to your mother and let her know where he is."

"I'll have to tell the Becketts about you. Mary will be working in the kitchen for her food and keep, but I don't know what they will say about two children."

"We'll work too," I said. "I can clean and Paul can help with the garden and the horses."

"If they could earn something for their work, we can all save enough for their mother's passage next spring," Mary said.

"After being alone three years, having a family to share my days will be better than having my pockets filled with gold." Nicholas hugged us.

Questions about *Journey to America—1848*

1. Why was Bridget's mother sending her children to Boston?

   _____

   _____

2. What hardships did people face on the voyage to America?

   _____

   _____

   _____

3. Why didn't the children stay with their Uncle James in Boston?

   _____

   _____

4. What kind of a person was Nicholas? Support your opinion with facts from the story.

   _____

   _____

   _____

5. How did Bridget say she and Paul could help?

   _____

   _____

6. Do you think a story like this could happen today? Why or why not?

   _____

   _____

Name_____

Journey to America—1848
Vocabulary

A. Read the definitions of the four similar words below. Then choose the correct word to complete each sentence.

    immigrate—(verb) to move from one country to another country to live
    immigrant—(noun) a person who moves from one country to another to live
    immigrants—(noun) people who move from one country to another to live
    immigration—(noun) the act of moving from one country to another to live

1. Paul and Bridget were _____ from Ireland.

2. Their mother planned to _____ to the United States later.

3. Uncle James was an _____ who had come from Ireland
    two years earlier.

4. _____ to the United States helped people in Ireland when
    the potato crop failed and they didn't have enough to eat.

B. Use these words from the story to complete the sentences below.

official	dock	deck	passengers	voyage
due	belongings	provisions	passage	

1. The _____ at the dock filled out the papers for Mary.

2. Nicholas paid the money that was _____.

3. The _____ had a long _____ to America.

4. The children's _____ on the ship was paid for with the money
    Uncle James had sent.

5. The passengers carried their _____ and _____ to

    living quarters below the _____.

6. They stood on the _____ and breathed the fresh air.

Name_____

Journey to America—1848

This Is Now

Write a letter to Bridget. Tell her about your community and school so she will know what life in the United States is like today.

_____
your street address

_____
your city and state

_____
date

Dear Bridget,

_____

_____

_____

_____

_____

_____

_____

_____

_____

Sincerely,

_____
your name

Journey to America—1848

A Tight Squeeze

In the 1840s, passengers traveling on sailing ships from Ireland to the United States were crowded into the hold of the ship. The number of passengers on the ships varied. Often there were 400 to 1,000 passengers living in the small space in the hold during the long voyage. The ships' captains received part of the money the passengers paid for their voyage. For that reason, the captains often crowded large numbers of passengers into the hold where products were usually carried.

Follow these directions to find out approximately how much space you would have if you were traveling in 1848 on a sailing ship from England to the United States.

1. If there were 600 passengers, you would have about three square feet of space. Cut four strings, each three feet in length. Arrange them in a square on the floor. That is the approximate space each person would have. Stand and sit in the space.

2. If there were 1,000 passengers, you would have about two square feet of space. Cut four strings, each two feet long. Arrange them in a square on the floor. That is the approximate space each person would have. Stand and sit in the space.

3. Everyone in the class will place their two-foot squares together on the playground. Sit in your square while you complete an activity (workbook page, an art lesson, math exercises, or eat a snack.) Write to tell how you felt while you were working or eating in that small space.

_____

_____

_____

_____

_____

_____

Jebediah's wide-brimmed hat shaded his eyes from the sun. He heard a horse gallop up to him.

"Quaker!" a man called out. "Did you see the runaways? There's a sweet reward for the return of these slaves."

Jebediah looked up at the man. "A fine horse thee has," he said. "The old mare in the barn is too old to pull heavy loads. Father has a mind to buy a new horse."

"This one is not for sale. If you turn those slaves over to me, I'll give you a share of the money, and I won't tell your pa. The slaves are a man and a boy about your age," the man said.

Jebediah shook his head. "They are not here. If thee would like to give thy horse a rest, Father will be back soon. I have to take vegetables to town before sundown."

"I've no time. Every slave-catcher this side of the river is looking for those runaways. If my partners and I don't find them on the road, we'll search all the Quaker barns and houses tonight."

"Good day to thee then," Jebediah said.

Jebediah walked into the barn and put his hand on the back of the brown mare. The horse followed Jebediah outside.

"It is too dangerous to wait for Father's return," Jebediah thought. Word had come yesterday that the two runaways were on their way. If they tried to come to the house for help, they would be caught and sent back. He had to find them and take them to another Friend's house.

Jebediah hitched a cart to the mare. He set a raised cover over the bottom of the cart and piled vegetables on top. There wasn't much room in the hidden compartment, but the runaways could manage.

"I'll take Sister Rebecca to Aunt Sarah's house," Jebediah thought. "No one will suspect anything if my six-year-old sister is riding with me." He hurried to the house.

"Thee won't mind if we go through the woods, Rebecca?" Jebediah asked.

She shook her head, but she looked worried as the cart bumped along the path.

"We will stop and pick some berries for Aunt Sarah. Thee shall have berries and cream for thy dinner."

They stopped near a berry patch and took two pails out of the cart. Jebediah couldn't tell Rebecca the real reason they were in the woods. If the slave-catchers stopped them, it was better she didn't know.

"Thee can start on this side of the berry patch," Jebediah said. "I'll go to another." Jebediah hurried down the path to the muddy riverbank. Vines covered the side of the bank. There were tunnels and a cave hidden under the vines. Runaways often stayed there during the day.

"This is the road!" Jebediah called. He heard someone crawling through the vines. "Follow quickly and climb into the wagon when I lift the cover. There is danger."

Jebediah ran to the wagon and lifted the cover. When he heard footsteps, he left the wagon to meet Rebecca.

"Did thee find ripe berries?" Jebediah asked.

"My pail is full," Rebecca answered.

"The river berries are green," Jebediah said, "but thee has enough. We must be on our way." Jebediah hurried in front of Rebecca and fastened the lid before she reached the wagon. He rearranged the vegetables.

Before they reached town, two men on horses galloped up beside them and pulled on the mare's reins. "Where are you headed?" one man asked.

"I'm going to see Aunt Sarah, and we are having berries and cream," Rebecca said.

"We're searching every wagon on the road," the other man said. He threw the vegetables out of the cart. "Get down! We are turning over the cart!"

Jebediah knew they would find the hollow space if they tipped over the wagon.

"Thee can't have my berries!" Rebecca started to cry. She stood between the men and the cart, clutching her pail.

Before the men could lift her out of the way, another man rode up. It was the slave-catcher who had talked to Jebediah earlier.

"I've been looking for you," he said, "and here you are wasting time with children. There are five Quaker wagons heading into town right now. They must be searched!"

Jebediah knew Mother had given Father his message. The Friends were trying to confuse the slave-catchers.

"We were almost caught," Rebecca said after the men rode off. "I cried as loud as I could."

"I don't know how thee knew, but this is the last time I try to keep a secret from thee," Jebediah said. "Thee and thy sweet freedom berries saved us all."

Name_____

Questions about *Freedom Berries*

1. Why did the visitor come to Jebediah's farm?

_____

_____

2. Why did Jebediah decide to look for the slaves before his father came home?

_____

_____

3. How did Rebecca keep the men from tipping over the wagon?

_____

_____

4. How did Father and the other Quaker Friends help Jebediah?

_____

_____

5. How did the runaways know that Jebediah had come to help them?

_____

_____

6. What clues in the story told you that Jebediah and his family had helped runaway slaves before?

_____

_____

_____

Freedom Berries
Vocabulary

Use the words in the Word Box to complete the crossword puzzle.

Across

2. to look carefully for something

4. the part of the hat that circles the head

5. another name for the religious group, the Society of Friends

9. the state of being able to make your own choices and decision

11. something hidden from others

12. the time of day when the sun disappears over the horizon

Down

1. fruit that grows on a vine

3. a space that is between two objects or sections

6. people fleeing slavery

7. another word for a Quaker

8. people who are owned by others

10. a female horse

Word Box		
secret	mare	freedom
runaways	brim	berries
search	sundown	Quakers
Friend	compartment	slaves

Name_____

Freedom Berries
What Happened Next?

Write part two of the *Freedom Berries* story. Tell what happened when Jebediah and Rebecca reached Aunt Sarah's house.

_____

_____

_____

_____

_____

_____

_____

_____

_____

_____

_____

_____

Name_____

Freedom Berries
The Underground Railroad

Quakers are members of a peaceful religious group. They believed that owning slaves was wrong. In the 1800s, before the Civil War, they helped many slaves travel from the southern states to the northern states and Canada so they could be free. Slave-catchers were people who captured runaway slaves. They were given rewards for returning the slaves to the slave holders.

The secret route that slaves traveled when they escaped was called the Underground Railroad. The houses and places where runaways were hidden and given food and shelter were called *stations.* People like Jebediah who helped them travel from one place to another were called *conductors.*

Use the information above to complete these sentences.

1. Jebediah's house was a _____ where slaves who had

   _____ were hidden.

2. Jebediah was a member of a religious group, The Society of Friends, who were also

   called _____.

3. _____ tried to capture the slaves and return them to

   their _____.

4. People who helped transport the slaves to freedom were called _____.

5. Slaves who escaped were called _____.

6. To be free, the slaves had to travel to the _____

   or _____.

7. _____ received _____ when they returned the slaves.

8. The _____ was not a railroad at all. It was a

   _____ that the slaves traveled to reach free states and Canada.

Spanish words to learn:
Pan de muertos *(pahn de mwer-tos)* – bread of the dead
El día de los muertos *(el día de los mwer-tos)* – Day of the Dead

Lisa looked out her bedroom window. She watched Elena and Mom carry suitcases into the house. Her cousin Elena was coming from Mexico for the rest of the school year. Her parents were sending her to the United States so she could practice her English. It was almost the end of October, so Elena had missed the first part of the school year.

"Sixth grade won't be much fun," Lisa thought. "I'll be doing homework all afternoon and evening. After I help Elena, I'll have to do mine. No more TV or visiting friends! At least Elena already speaks English so we can talk to each other."

Mom had insisted that Lisa give up her activities after school. "I can't drive back and forth all day," Mom had said. "I have to pick you both up right after school. It wouldn't be fair to have Elena wait an hour for you to finish play practice."

Lisa had a big part in the school play *Let's Celebrate.* She hadn't yet told Mr. Blake, the director, that she couldn't come to rehearsals. She was hoping Mom would change her mind.

Mom put the suitcases by Elena's bed. "Well, here we are," she said. "I'll leave you two together to get acquainted. Lisa, you can help Elena unpack."

"Mom, let me help with dinner," Lisa pleaded.

"Not tonight," Mom said, "Dad will bring pizza." She left the room.

"I'm glad you are in my room," Elena said. "My sisters and I do everything together. We'll be good friends, no?"

"We'll be together a lot," Lisa answered. "Let's unpack."

Elena opened the big suitcase. "I brought things for the Day of the Dead, *El día de los muertos,*" she said. She took out pictures and candles. "They're for your family. My mother sent them. You can fix an altar for our grandfather."

"We don't celebrate the Day of the Dead," Lisa said.

"But I saw all the skeletons in the windows on our way from the airport."

"The skeletons are for Halloween," Lisa explained. "It's a fun time for kids. Mom told me about The Day of the Dead in Mexico, but I didn't understand all of it. Some of her friends have altars in their houses for members of their families who have died. Mom doesn't. My dad is from England, so it's different in our house."

Elena set the pictures and candles on the dresser. "Everything will be strange here," she said. Lisa helped Elena put her clothes away.

"I'll miss being with my family for The Day of the Dead holidays. We invite the souls of our ancestors and family who have died to visit us. The cemetery is cleaned up and decorated with marigolds and other flowers. We leave food at home and in the cemetery to honor the dead. It begins on the last day of October and ends on the second day of November. Look, I brought candy to share."

Elena showed Lisa a box of sugar skeletons and chocolate skulls. "You can give them to your mother to save," Elena said. "I have *pan de muertos* too. My mother baked the bread and I decorated it with the bones."

Lisa looked at the frosting bones and skull. "It looks good. Let's show this to Mom," Lisa said. Elena followed Lisa downstairs.

"Mom, Elena brought these things for Day of the Dead," Lisa said. "It's a special holiday for her."

Mom looked at the pictures, candles, and treats. She put her arm around Elena. "We could have an altar. I would like to remember my dad. Some of our neighbors set up altars on the first day of November."

Lisa and Elena watched Mom arrange the candles and pictures on a cabinet. "On *El día de los muertos*, we'll put out foods your grandpa liked. We could invite friends to share dinner with us. I've lived here a long time and sometimes I forget about Mexican holidays, but many Mexican Americans celebrate them here. I always watch the parades and dancing on Cinco de Mayo, and I'd like to celebrate more special days."

"Mom, while we're talking about holidays, Elena should learn about the ones we celebrate in the United States like Thanksgiving and the Fourth of July. The school play is about all the holidays in the year. Elena could be in the play. She could find out about our holidays and really practice English!"

"I'd really like that. Could I?" Elena asked.

"Well, Mom?" Lisa asked.

"I'll pick you both up from school after rehearsals at 4:00 p.m., if Mr. Blake agrees," Mom said.

Name_____

Questions about *Let's Celebrate*

1. Why was Elena coming to the United States?

_____

_____

2. Give two reasons why Lisa wasn't sure she would enjoy Elena's visit.

_____

_____

3. Why did Lisa's mom change her mind about Lisa taking part in the play?

_____

_____

4. Describe how Elena's family celebrated the Day of the Dead.

_____

_____

_____

5. Many cultures have special days to remember those who have died. Why do you think these holidays exist? What is the name given to that day in the United States?

_____

_____

_____

_____

Name_____

Let's Celebrate

Antonyms

Antonyms are words with opposite meanings. Find an antonym in the story for each word below. The number following each word tells you the paragraph in which the antonym can be found.

1. shut (10) _____

2. remember (20) _____

3. familiar (14) _____

4. disagrees (24) _____

5. enemies (8) _____

6. separated (9) _____

7. short (20) _____

8. begins (15) _____

9. before (24) _____

Word Meaning

Write each word in the Word Box next to its meaning.

Word Box			
cemetery	holiday	celebrate	cabinet
altar	arrange	soul	rehearsals

1. the spirit of a person _____

2. a place where the dead are buried _____

3. a day of celebration _____

4. a piece of furniture with shelves and/or drawers _____

5. practice times for a play _____

6. to take part in a special occasion _____

7. a special place to pray or honor ancestors _____

8. to put in a special order _____

Name_____

Let's Celebrate

Comparing Holidays

The story provided information about how the people of Mexico celebrate *El día de los muertos*. Use the Venn diagram below to compare this holiday with the holiday of Halloween as it is celebrated in the United States.

Write words or phrases that fit each section of the diagram. You do not need to use complete sentences. Two examples have been done for you.

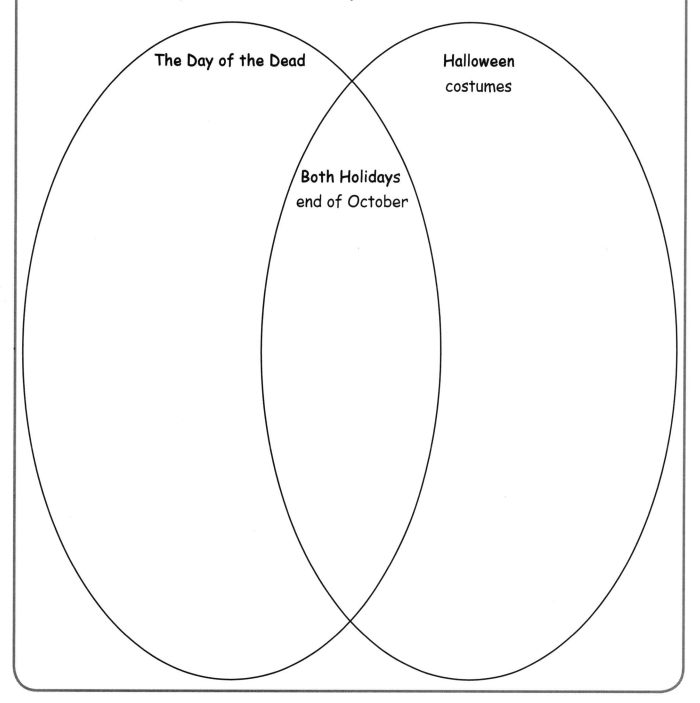

The Day of the Dead

Halloween
costumes

Both Holidays
end of October

Name_____

Let's Celebrate
Helping Verbs

A. Many verbs are action words like *run, jump,* and *sing.* Sometimes helping verbs like *was, will, were, have,* and *has* are paired with an action word to make the meaning clearer and set the time of the action.

> In the sentence *I will bake the cake, bake* is the action word and *will* tells the reader that the action will take place in the future.
>
> In the sentence *I had baked the cake, had* makes it clear that the cake was baked in the past.

Read each sentence below. Draw one line under the action verb. Draw two lines under the helping verb.

1. I have finished the work.

2. She had not told Mr. Blake.

3. Elena had missed the first part of the school year.

4. We will celebrate tomorrow.

5. Dad will bring pizza.

B. Helping verbs are sometimes written in a contracted form. For example, *I will leave* can be written *I'll leave.* Rewrite these sentences using the correct contracted form.

will = *'ll*   have = *'ve*

1. I will bring pizza.

_____

2. You have done a good job.

_____

3. I have finished my homework.

_____

4. He will be home soon.

_____

One soft summer night Grandma and I sat on the porch swing. We were simply swinging—legs hanging free, while the gentle breeze of almost night ruffled our hair. It was then that I saw the star. It was the first star of evening, and I squeezed Grandma's arm and made a silent wish. Grandma looked up and smiled slowly, but there was something in her eyes that wasn't smiling. "What is it, Grandma? What's the matter?"

Grandma gazed back at the star, drew a shaky breath, and sighed. "I was just remembering Leah."

"Leah? Is she one of your friends?" I asked.

Grandma took my hand in hers. Her skin was cool and firm. Her eyes looked at me, but they seemed to focus on something or someone far beyond. "Leah," she said and her voice caught for a moment. "Leah was my best friend. It was in the old country. We were very young. I remember her thick brown hair and big brown eyes. You should have heard us giggle." Then Grandma stopped. A single tear slid down her cheek.

"Grandma, what happened? Where's Leah now?" I searched her face for answers. I had never seen her like this. Grandma came to America from France during World War II. She spoke lovingly about her mother and father, but seldom said anything else. "Grandma, where's Leah?"

"Leah…I don't know where Leah is. The last time I saw her…." Grandma stopped again. She looked up at that one yellow star in the sky. She squeezed my hand. "Leah was wearing a yellow star on her coat. Leah's parents were Jewish. When the Nazi soldiers occupied France, all the Jews had to wear yellow stars. Leah's mother had sewn the star to Leah's coat. When I asked if I could have one too, she said, 'Stars belong in the sky. When people take them down, trouble is near.' I didn't understand then. I don't really understand even today."

Grandma sighed and squeezed my hand. Then she continued, "It wasn't long after that day that the soldiers started taking everyone who wore a yellow star away. They were taken to camps. We left too. Mama and Papa brought me here to America. They said that France wasn't safe. We started a new life…but the soldiers had taken Leah and her family. I never saw her again. I don't know what happened to her."

Grandma shook her head as if to erase a bad thought. "Terrible things happened in the camps, but there were survivors…there were a few survivors." Grandma shook her head again.

She stood up and leaned on the porch railing. "It's times like this—still, silent, almost night with yellow stars in the sky that I remember her most. Do you suppose she survived? Do you suppose she's out there somewhere? Or do you think…."

Grandma turned and opened the door to go inside. She looked back at the darkening sky. "Yellow stars—they belong in the sky."

Name_____

Questions about *The Yellow Stars*

A. List characteristics to show what you know about the characters.

Grandma

_____

_____

_____

Leah

_____

_____

_____

Narrator

_____

_____

_____

B. When Grandma asked the questions near the end of the story, did she expect an answer? Why or why not?

_____

_____

_____

_____

Name_____

The Yellow Stars
Vocabulary

Read the nonfiction account of **antisemitism** below. Use a dictionary to find the meaning for each underlined word. Write the meanings on the back of this page.

Approximately 11 million people were killed because of Nazi genocidal policy during World War II. It was a goal of Hitler's regime to create a European world both dominated and populated by the "Aryan" race. The Nazis wanted to eliminate millions of people they deemed undesirable. Jewish people fell into this category.

In 1933 German Jews were no longer allowed to enter cinemas, theaters, swimming pools, and resorts. The publishing of Jewish newspapers was suspended. Jews were required to carry identification cards and wear Star of David badges. One night, Nazis burned synagogues and vandalized Jewish businesses. Next, Jewish children were barred from schools. Curfews restricted travel, and Jews were banned from public places. Germany began to expel Jews from within its borders.

In 1939 Hitler turned to the remaining European Jewish population. He relocated Jewish families into ghettos in eastern Europe. Simultaneously, mobile squads killed millions of Jewish people. The next step was to send Jews to concentration and death camps. Approximately 6 million people died for one reason: they were Jewish.

Celebrating Diversity • EMC 798

The Yellow Stars

Feelings

A. Grandma's feelings changed as she told her story about Leah. Write a sentence to tell how you think Grandma felt:

1. Before she began telling her story

_____

_____

_____

2. As she told her story

_____

_____

_____

3. After she finished telling her story

_____

_____

_____

B. What clues in the story helped you know how Grandma felt?

_____

_____

_____

_____

The Yellow Stars

Memories

Speak with an older relative or friend. Ask that person to tell you about a memory of his or her childhood. Use this form to record the responses and then think about them.

What was the memory?

_____

_____

_____

How did the person feel about the memory?

_____

_____

_____

Did you notice changes in facial features, gestures, or voice as the person spoke?

_____

_____

Write a paragraph that describes your conversation.

_____

_____

_____

_____

Photo © Courtesy LPGA

Eight-year-old Nancy Lopez was bored with trailing her parents around the golf course. It was 1965, and Nancy's mother, Marina, had been told by a doctor to exercise regularly. So each day Marina and Nancy's father, Domingo, played golf at Cahoon Park in Roswell, New Mexico. Nancy went along.

Finally, Nancy asked her parents if she could play too. Domingo handed her one of Marina's clubs. He gave her a few quick pointers, but there was little time for a real lesson. Another group of golfers was playing behind them.

Whack! Whack! Whack! Off she went, knocking the ball across the grass. She labored to keep up with her parents and to stay ahead of the other golfers. Every day they played. Before many months passed, Nancy learned to send the ball rocketing down the course, over the heads of her startled parents.

Domingo taught her the strokes she needed and when to use various clubs. She practiced daily with Marina's adult-sized clubs. They were too big, but Nancy loved golf, and her game got better and better.

As most parents do, Domingo and Marina wanted a lot for Nancy and her older sister. They did all they could to help Nancy's game. They realized that the course at Cahoon Park had no sand traps. These are large sandy spots that make golf courses more challenging. Domingo dug a huge hole in the backyard and filled it with sand. This way Nancy could practice hitting her ball out of a sand trap.

Domingo taught her all that he knew about golf. He coached her through problems and cheered her successes.

The Lopez family didn't have a lot of money, and golf was an expensive sport. Marina and Domingo worked hard and denied themselves many things. In part, they did this so Nancy could compete in the sport she loved.

When she was nine, Nancy competed in the state Pee Wee tournament and won! In fact her score was so low she would still have won if she'd competed against the older kids. (In golf, the lowest score wins.)

She was eleven the first time she outscored her father in a game of golf. It was a close game, and they were both proud of her accomplishment. Years later, Domingo still had her score card from that day displayed in his office.

When she was only twelve, Nancy amazed everyone by winning the state Women's Amateur tournament, in which she competed against adults. She went on to win the U.S. Golf Association's national competition for junior girls twice.

Nancy lit up golf courses with her shining smile and warm, friendly calm. She made it look as if being a champion was easy, but it was not. She worked very hard and faced many barriers.

At her high school there was no golf team for girls. Nancy wanted to play on the boys' team, but the school refused to allow it. She was disappointed, but determined. Then, with an attorney's help, Nancy again asked to play on the boys' team. This time the school allowed her to try out. It was a good decision. With Nancy on the team, the school took the state championship two years in a row.

The Lopez family had to overcome racial prejudice as well. Most people warmed to Nancy's bright smile and practiced game, but not all. Some of the competitions Nancy wanted to play in required a country club sponsor. The club in Roswell didn't want the Mexican American Lopez family as members. But a country club in Albuquerque did. They were grateful for the chance to make Nancy's family honorary members.

By 1977 everyone knew that Nancy Lopez had a bright future in professional golf. She was twenty-one when she turned pro. "Turning pro" means playing in tournaments that offer money prizes. She wanted to help pay back her family for all they had done for her. She especially wanted to buy Marina a new house.

In her first year as a professional golfer, Nancy played well. In fact she placed second in several tournaments. Then, tragically, Marina Lopez died from an infection following an operation. It was a terrible shock.

This was a hard time for the Lopez family. Nancy took some time off from golf. When she came back her game was not as effective as she wanted it to be. She thought about her mother a lot. Domingo told her to just let things happen.

Things did. In 1978 Nancy Lopez blew through the world of professional golf like a warm, friendly wind. She shattered records, winning five tournaments in a row. In all, she won nine tournaments that year. Young Nancy was named Rookie of the Year and Player of the Year.

Nancy Lopez has become a wife and mother, and golf has to share her with a larger family now. But she is still a winner. Her calm, her smile, and her hard work are well known all over the world.

Questions about *Nancy Lopez and Family*

1. How old was Nancy the first time she won a game of golf with her father?

_____

2. Why do you think this event was important to Nancy and Domingo?

_____

_____

3. What obstacles did Nancy face as a young golfer?

_____

_____

_____

4. Right after her mother's death, Nancy wasn't able to play as well as she wanted to. Why do you think this happened?

_____

_____

5. After reading this story, what can you tell about Nancy Lopez's personality? What clues helped you come to this conclusion?

_____

_____

_____

6. Why do you think the author entitled this selection *Nancy Lopez and Family*?

_____

_____

Nancy Lopez and Family
Vocabulary

A. Write an **antonym**, or opposite, for the underlined word in each sentence. Then write a sentence using the antonym. Use these words to help you.

unskilled   failures   amateur   leading

1. There is usually a crowd of fans <u>trailing</u> Nancy. _____

   _____

2. <u>Professional</u> golfers compete for cash prizes. _____

   _____

3. Nancy's father is proud of her <u>accomplishments</u>. _____

   _____

4. It was Nancy's <u>practiced</u> golf game that won tournaments. _____

   _____

B. The words below are all formed from the base word *compete*. Use them to complete the sentences.

competitive   competitors   competed   competition

1. Ray and Li are both _____ in the drawing contest.

2. The poem that wins the _____ will be published in the paper.

3. She is a very _____ athlete who is always trying her best to win.

4. When she was just twelve, Nancy _____ against adults.

Nancy Lopez and Family
Getting Help Along the Way

From the beginning, Nancy loved playing golf. What things do you love doing?

_____

_____

_____

Nancy's family was very important in helping her become a winning golfer. Write a paragraph about someone who has helped you achieve a goal.

_____

_____

_____

_____

Have you ever helped someone do something? Write a paragraph or more about what happened and how you felt.

_____

_____

_____

_____

_____

Nancy Lopez and Family
The Language of Golf

Unscramble the golf terms below. Then write the number of each word in front of the sentence that tells what it means.

1. ddasser _____

2. diedac _____

3. utpter _____

4. llagyer _____

5. rhogu _____

6. ngere _____

7. eet _____

8. ehlo _____

_____ A golfer uses a <u>putter</u> to hit the ball a short way across the green.

_____ The area on a golf course that is not mowed or landscaped is called the <u>rough</u>. If a golfer hits a ball into the rough, it can be hard to hit it out again.

_____ In golf the word <u>hole</u> describes the little hole in the ground that golfers try to hit the ball into. <u>Hole</u> also describes the sections, or divisions, of a golf course. Most golf courses have either 9 or 18 holes.

_____ Fans that stand on the edge of the golf course to watch a tournament are called the <u>gallery</u>.

_____ A <u>caddie</u> helps a golfer by giving advice and handling the golf clubs.

_____ The drive toward each hole begins at the <u>tee</u>. There, golfers hit the first stroke. The little wooden peg that golfers place the ball on is also called a <u>tee</u>.

_____ How you <u>address</u> the ball, or stand before hitting it, is very important.

_____ On the closely mowed <u>green</u>, golfers try to putt (hit) the ball into the hole.

Author Laurence Yep grew up in a world of cereal boxes, raw liver, pickles in a barrel, soda bottles, and penny bubble gum. His parents owned a grocery store in San Francisco. They lived very close to work. Their apartment on the corner of Pierce and Eddy Streets was above the store.

Everyone in the family worked in the grocery store. Laurence and his brother stocked shelves, sorted bottles, and flattened boxes. Prices needed to be marked on groceries. When the family could leave the store, they enjoyed picnics and other outdoor activities. Mr. Yep made butterfly kites and the family flew them. They went to the beach to wade in the water and gather sand. Mr. Yep built a sandbox on the roof of their apartment building. It was there that Laurence created his first imaginary kingdoms.

Laurence's parents felt that a good education was very important. They read to their children and had their children read to them. Laurence's favorite stories took place in the Land of Oz. He searched for the books in the library and read them all. Next he read every science fiction book he could find. He understood how the characters felt. They were thrust into strange worlds where they didn't belong. That was how he felt about being Chinese and American.

Laurence's parents were Chinese American. His father was born in China. He came to the United States at the age of ten. Laurence's mother was born in Ohio. She was raised in West Virginia and California.

Many Chinese Americans lived in the Chinatown district of San Francisco. They kept many Chinese customs and often spoke Chinese. They weren't always welcome in other neighborhoods. But the Yep family lived in another part of town. They would visit friends and relatives in Chinatown. Laurence felt more American than Chinese when he was growing up. But sometimes he felt that he didn't belong in either culture. Many of his stories reflect these feelings. They are about people who must learn to adjust to new places and people with different customs.

One of Laurence's early writing experiences was with the Junior Boys' Club. They wrote, acted in, and produced their own plays. They had to sell the tickets too. The money they earned helped pay for their club activities.

Laurence went to a Catholic school in Chinatown. He excelled in most subjects, but he didn't like learning Chinese. Most of his friends spoke Chinese at home and were in advanced classes. He had to take the beginning class.

When Laurence started high school, he stopped working long hours in the store. His parents wanted him to study. Laurence wanted to study chemistry in college. He did well in his English writing classes too. English won out over chemistry. Laurence decided to study journalism in college.

At Marquette University in Wisconsin, Laurence was homesick for San Francisco. He did well in all of his classes except journalism. His teacher suggested that he might do better writing fiction than reporting the facts. His teacher was right. Laurence wrote his first science fiction story "The Selchey Kids." He sold it to a magazine and was paid a penny a word.

At Marquette, Laurence met Joanne Ryder, a student editor for a school magazine. She introduced him to children's books. Joanne later became an editor for a book publisher. She asked Laurence to send her a children's story. He wrote *Sweetwater*, a science fiction story. It was published.

Laurence continued writing books for children and young adults. He has won many awards for books about Chinese Americans. Laurence Yep and Joanne Ryder are now married. Today they are both well-known authors for young people.

> **Have You Read Some of Laurence Yep's Award-Winning Books?**
>
> *The Lost Garden*
> *Child of the Owl*
> *Thief of Hearts*
> *Later Alligator*
> *The Rainbow People*
> *Tongues of Jade*
> *Dragonwings (1975)
> *Dragon's Gate (1993)
> *Mountain Light*
> *The Serpent's Children*
> *Sweetwater*
> *Kind Hearts and Gentle Monsters*
> *Newbery Honor Winners

Name_____

Questions about *Laurence Yep*

1. How did Laurence's parents influence his eventual career as an author?

_____

_____

_____

2. Why do you think Laurence felt more American than Chinese?

_____

_____

_____

3. What kind of books did Laurence most like to read? Why?

_____

_____

4. How do many of Laurence Yep's stories reflect his experiences growing up?

_____

_____

_____

5. Why didn't Laurence pursue a career in journalism?

_____

_____

Laurence Yep

Vocabulary

The words in the Word Box identify people and tell what they do. Write each word on the line in front of its definition.

Word Box					
journalist	grocer	parent	participant	student	citizen
spectator	philosopher	teacher	author	editor	

1. _____ a person who helps a writer prepare a book or story for publishing

2. _____ a person who sells food

3. _____ a person who studies thought and knowledge

4. _____ a person who takes part in an activity

5. _____ a person who belongs to a nation

6. _____ a person who watches an activity

7. _____ a person who attends a school

8. _____ a person who helps people learn

9. _____ a person who writes books and stories

10. _____ a person who is a mother or a father

11. _____ a person who gathers news and writes about it

Name_____

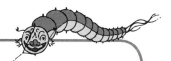

Laurence Yep
Writing About It

Laurence Yep and other authors invent characters and the worlds in which they live. Use the form below to invent a setting and characters for a story.

The Setting

Landscape/Geography

Housing and Buildings

The Characters

Clothes

Customs

Food

Entertainment

★Bonus: On another sheet of paper, write a story about visiting this world. Include the problems you would have there. That is the plot. How do you solve the problems? Illustrate your new world.

Name_____

Laurence Yep
The Chinese Language

The Chinese language is spoken by more people than any other language in the world. There are many dialects or different ways of speaking Chinese. Some dialects are so different that not all people speaking Chinese understand each other. Even though the dialects are different, Chinese-speaking people around the world can read the same Chinese writing.

Written Chinese words are characters or "pictures." They are written in columns from the top to the bottom of the page. The columns start on the right side of the page and move to the left.

Practice writing these Chinese characters for the word *friend.*
Remember to draw the strokes or parts of the characters in the order shown.

Trace	Copy
朋 友	

My Great-Grandmother Bonnie

My great-grandma Bonnie is ninety-two years old. I am ten and three-quarters. Grandma Bonnie and I like to play a story game. We play it all afternoon. Grandma Bonnie always starts with a terrifically long sentence.

"When I was ten and three-quarters years old… the winds were still and hot, and the humidity in the air made me feel like I was swimming in my own backyard even as the sun began to set; my mother would give me ten cents so I could walk to town and buy an ice-cream cone and a bag of popcorn to eat while I listened to a band play from the band wagon that parked outside the bank on Saturday nights."

"Once I listened to a band play on an enormous stage equipped with wireless microphones, two-story-high speakers, neon lights, and billowy smoke. They didn't serve ice-cream cones or popcorn, but that's okay because it would have cost a lot more than ten cents."

"When I was ten and three-quarters years old… I was in the fifth grade, and every weekday morning I jumped onto the wagon that stopped outside our house. Then the driver drove the horses right to the middle of town. All of us West End kids had to go to school in the basement of the Garrett Library because there wasn't room for us in the schoolhouse."

"Hey Grandma, I'm in the fifth grade too. I ride a loud yellow bus to my brand new school. I don't think there could ever be too many kids to fit in my school. I hope not, because our town library doesn't have a basement."

"When I was ten and three-quarters years old… I lived with my mom and my dad and my two brothers and my two sisters at 1301 West Quincy Street. It was a large house that my father built of wood. Downstairs it had a kitchen, a living room, a dining room, and two bedrooms. Upstairs it had three bedrooms. And outdoors is where we went to the privy."

"I live at 153 Cottage Court with my mom and my brother. We have a lot of rooms too. And we go to the bathroom indoors."

"When I was ten and three-quarters years old… I helped my father hoe potatoes and weed onions. I helped him chop wood to use in our cookstove. I gathered eggs from the chickens and helped the ice man carry a big block of ice to our icebox. Some days I helped Mother sew underclothes, cook a meal, or wash laundry on the washboard."

"I planted a garden with Mom this summer. Sometimes I bake cookies or throw my laundry into the machine. But I definitely do not sew my own underwear, and my refrigerator works quite nicely without a block of ice."

"When I was ten and three-quarters years old… I got sick with a sore throat. My mother made me gargle with salt and pepper and vinegar. Then she wrapped a bacon strip around my neck. Sometimes my cat would chew on the bacon wrapped around my neck!"

"When I have a sore throat, my mom gives me herbal tea and pink medicine. I lie on the couch all day and watch TV and play video games."

"When I was ten and three-quarters years old… my favorite time of day was when Father came home from the fields. One night, when he was chasing us kids around the house on his hands and knees, my little brother picked up a wooden spoon and hit him over the head. A big knot came to Father's head, and that was the end of that game!"

"We play basketball when we go to Dad's house. My little brother hasn't hit Dad on the head with the ball yet. Dad always catches it."

When she starts to tell me about something Great-Great-Grandpa Miller taught her how to do, I know the story game is almost over.

"When I was ten and three-quarters years old… my father taught me how to make a kite with sticks from the yard, old newspapers, and paste made of flour and water."

"Will you show me how to make a kite?"

Sometimes it isn't a kite. Sometimes it is homemade ice cream or wooden cars or clothespin dolls. But Grandma's answer is always the same, "YES, I WILL!"

Name_____

Questions about *My Great-Grandmother Bonnie*

1. In this story a ten-year-old girl and her great-grandmother play a story game.
   Explain the story game.

   _____

   _____

   _____

   _____

2. The woman in this story has lived for ninety-two years. What are some of the changes
   hinted at in this story that she has seen the world go through during her lifetime?

   _____

   _____

   _____

   _____

3. What were some of the great-grandmother's chores as a child? What are some of the
   girl's chores?

   _____

   _____

   _____

4. At the end of the story game, the girl and her great-grandmother make a kite. Do you think
   the girl knew they would complete a project together? Explain your answer.

   _____

   _____

   _____

My Great-Grandmother Bonnie
Vocabulary

A. Use a dictionary to find the meanings of these words from the story.
Write the meanings on the lines.

1. terrifically _____

2. humidity _____

3. enormous _____

4. equipped _____

5. neon _____

6. billowy _____

7. definitely _____

8. gargle _____

9. herbal _____

B. Using hints from the story, describe the following items that are <u>not</u> common in today's world.

1. washboard _____

_____

2. privy _____

_____

Name_____

My Great-Grandmother Bonnie
Ask Great-Grandma Bonnie

1. In this story the old woman described some aspects of her childhood during the early part of the twentieth century. Write five specific questions you would like to ask Great-Grandma Bonnie about life so long ago.

    Question 1:

    _____

    Question 2:

    _____

    Question 3:

    _____

    Question 4:

    _____

    Question 5:

    _____

2. Would you or would you not like to have Great-Grandma Bonnie as your own great-grandmother? Explain your answer.

    _____

    _____

    _____

3. Tell about a positive experience you have had with an elderly person.

    _____

    _____

    _____

Name_____

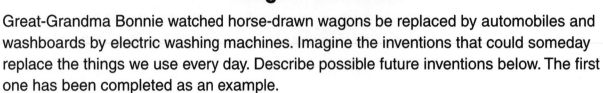

My Great-Grandmother Bonnie
Imagine the Future

Great-Grandma Bonnie watched horse-drawn wagons be replaced by automobiles and washboards by electric washing machines. Imagine the inventions that could someday replace the things we use every day. Describe possible future inventions below. The first one has been completed as an example.

1. Cars might be replaced by <u>flying machines that require no gas and run on water.</u>

2. Washing machines might be replaced by _____

_____

3. Fresh foods might be replaced by _____

_____

4. Books might be replaced by _____

_____

5. Staircases might be replaced by _____

_____

6. Wood might be replaced by _____

_____

7. Fossil fuels might be replaced by _____

_____

8. Money might be replaced by _____

_____

A **powwow** is a Native American celebration of culture and pride. Powwows are held all over the United States year-round. Powwows take place in small towns and large cities. They happen on reservations and in parks and at fairgrounds. Sometimes only a few families gather for a powwow. Other times, thousands of people celebrate together. A powwow may be held in honor of a new baby or a good harvest. It may be just in celebration of life. It may continue for several hours or a few days.

The Drum

The *Drum* is the lifeblood of a powwow. The Drum has two meanings. It is an actual drum and also the singers and dancers who perform around it. The Drum is located at the center of the arena. The dancers are colorfully dressed in beads and feathers. Their skin may be painted. Their costumes may include bells, bones, leather, and cloth of many bright and beautiful colors. A dancer's clothing may tell something about the tribe's heritage. The drum itself is colorful too. A rawhide pad is stretched over a painted three- to four-foot-tall wooden base.

The Drum performs hours of songs and dances. Custom says that each song must be different. No song is repeated even when a powwow lasts three or four days.

Many types of dances are performed. There are grass dances, traditional dances, jingle dress dances, and gourd dances. Some are formal and ceremonial. Some are performed just for fun. The Head Man and Lady of the Drum dance first. Then soon, many powwow participants join in. Some singers and dancers who are part of a Drum travel from powwow to powwow. At each stop they entertain a whole new crowd.

Special Dances and Ceremonies

Some of the songs and dances at a powwow have special rules. When a blanket song is played, people at a powwow contribute gifts (usually money) before joining in the dance. When the Drum plays a war dance, dancers are not allowed to take a break until they all take a break together.

During a give-away ceremony, a special family is honored. The honored family dances in a circle. Others offer the family gifts and join in the dance. Finally, the honored family shares a gift with someone they would like to honor.

Contests

Many powwow dancers enter a competition. The dancers' costumes are judged. Songs with unusual rhythms and breaks test the dancing ability. The number of dances a contestant dances is considered too. Many levels of competition are available. If you are old enough to dance, you are old enough to enter a contest. Singers also enter into competition at a powwow. Sometimes contests revolve around crafts and games too.

The Crafts Fair

Often a crafts fair is located just outside the arena. Here elders share stories and skills with the younger generations. Many Native American artworks are offered for sale.

Paintings and jewelry found at a powwow's crafts fair often use natural materials such as sand, plant dyes, stones, seeds, and shells. They also include many bright colors and distinct symbols. The colors and symbols used in Native American art often tell a story. Many of the stories show a deep respect for animal and plant life and for the beauty of the natural world.

Native American Games and Goodies

Sometimes old traditional games are played near the crafts fair. Many of these use game pieces from nature such as stones and tree limbs. The game's rules are usually simple. Young children and older people play the games together.

Traditional Native American foods are also offered in the crafts fair area. Many of the foods are made with corn and wheat. Fry bread is a favorite with the children because it is sweet and crisp.

Name_____

Questions about *Dancing to the Drum*

1. How does a powwow celebrate the pride and culture of Native Americans?

_____

_____

2. What are some reasons that powwows are celebrated?

_____

_____

3. What is the Drum and its importance at a powwow?

_____

_____

_____

4. Why do you think Native American art includes so many symbols representing different aspects of nature?

_____

_____

5. Fill in the circles below with phrases and symbols to indicate what happens in each area of a powwow.

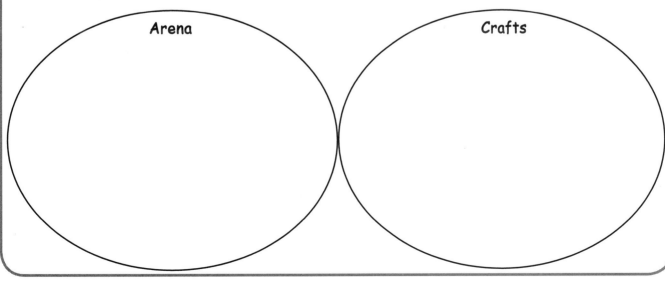

Arena

Crafts

Name_____

Dancing to the Drum
Synonyms

Write the number of each word on the line in front of its synonym.

1. heritage	_____ clear
2. distinct	_____ praise
3. custom	_____ inheritance
4. competition	_____ tradition
5. honor	_____ art
6. craft	_____ contest
7. contestant	_____ competitor

Complete the Sentences

Use these words from the story to complete the sentences below.

harvest   reservation   respect   celebration   ceremonial

1. My Native American friend, Tala, lives on a _____ that was granted her tribe by the United States government.

2. Kelly performed a formal _____ dance that honored her ancestors.

3. Recycling soda cans and picking up litter shows you have _____ for your environment.

4. Sam's birthday _____ included cake, ice cream, and lots of presents.

5. I will organize a fall _____ party to celebrate the abundant crops we brought in this year.

 Celebrating Diversity • EMC 798

Dancing to the Drum
Comparing Celebrations

1. Would you enjoy attending a powwow? Why or why not?

_____

_____

_____

_____

2. Compare a Native American powwow to a celebration or an event you have attended.
How are the two events alike? How are they different?

_____

_____

_____

_____

_____

_____

_____

_____

_____

_____

Name_____

Dancing to the Drum
Planning a Cultural Celebration

If you were to plan a festival to celebrate your own culture, you would have to think about what foods, songs, games, stories, and other events and ideas make your culture unique. Answer the questions below as you pretend to plan your own cultural celebration.

1. What will you call your festival?

   _____

2. What songs that are common to your culture will you have sung at your festival?

   _____

   _____

3. What fairy tales, poems, tall tales, or stories that are common to your culture will you have told at your festival?

   _____

   _____

4. What crafts or styles of art that are common to your culture will you display or teach at your festival?

   _____

   _____

5. Describe the style of clothing that symbolizes your culture.

   _____

   _____

6. What foods that are common to your culture will you offer at your festival?

   _____

7. On another sheet of paper, draw a picture of the layout of your festival, showing what activities will take place and where each one will be located.

Photo by Hugh Kidd

On January 2, 1999, Corine Bowie Bunn celebrated her ninetieth birthday with ninety-seven friends and family members. The mayor of Oakland, California, Elihu M. Harris, proclaimed January 2, Corine Bunn Day. President Bill Clinton and Hillary Rodham Clinton sent birthday wishes. Guests honored Corine with speeches and poems. There were lots of memories to celebrate. Many people came that night to thank her for all she had given to the community for over fifty years.

Since Corine and her family moved to Oakland in 1947, she has sewn clothes and hats, made quilts, crocheted, and baked for others. Whenever help was needed, Corine volunteered. She sang in two choirs at the Solid Rock Baptist Church and was a member of the Ruth Circle, a group that helped people in the church and in the community.

Corine had been a second mother to many of her children's high school friends. She opened her heart and her home when they needed help. She prepared extra food so the young visitors could have a hot meal. They came to her when they had no one else to help them. Corine listened to their problems and cheered their achievements.

After her children were grown, Corine didn't stop helping children. She was the family baby-sitter for all of her grandchildren while their parents worked.

Corine became president of the West Oakland Neighborhood Senior Citizens group. The group helped each other and watched over neighborhood children. They had sewing and cooking classes. She helped plan activities the elderly could enjoy.

Corine loves to tell stories about growing up in Arkansas.

Growing-up Years

Corine Bowie and her twin sister Irean were born in Locust Bayou, Arkansas, in 1909. The twins were the descendants of black slaves, Native Americans, and white settlers. Corine's grandmother, Sally Bowie, had a Native American mother. Her white father was a slave owner. Sally was raised in her father's household. She was a young woman in 1865 when the black slaves in the United States were set free.

Sally told the twins stories about her life while she taught them how to quilt. The quilts were made from clothing the family had worn. When there was a bad storm or the twins were frightened, they wrapped the quilts around themselves or hid under them. Since the pieces of cloth had come from others in the family, it made them feel that the family was there with them, keeping them safe.

Corine's mother, Lillie, died when Corine was seven. Her father, Lee, couldn't care for the young twins and their four brothers and sisters without help from his family. Grandma Sally, his mother, was a midwife who delivered babies in neighboring communities. She couldn't care for Corine and Irean because she traveled. Uncle Charlie, Lee's brother, took the girls into his home.

Charlie and his wife, Carrie, lived on a farm. They raised cotton, sugarcane, vegetables, fruit, and peanuts. They grew or made almost everything they needed. Aunt Carrie sewed most of their clothes, but sometimes she ordered outfits from the Sears catalog.

They raised horses, cows, chickens, and hogs. The twins helped care for the animals. Irean milked the cows while Corine held the bucket. There were more chickens than anything else. They wandered all over the farm—even into the house! It was so hot in the summer that many hens died from the heat while they sat on their eggs. On cold winter days the twins built bonfires outdoors to warm the feet of the cows so their feet wouldn't freeze. Corine managed to stay warm by carrying hot baked potatoes in her pockets.

Every Sunday the family walked to church or rode in a horse-drawn wagon. They spent the whole day in church. They went to prayer meetings during the week. "People said my daddy was the prayingest man there was," Corine explained.

Molasses cakes were a treat the whole family enjoyed. One day Irean and Corine were in charge of the house while their aunt and uncle were working in the fields. They decided to make a molasses cake for dinner. Corine measured out the flour and the other ingredients. When Irean started to pour the molasses, all the syrup spilled into the bowl. Corine mixed in all the flour she could find. She poured the batter into every pan in the house and baked the cakes.

"Did you fix anything to eat?" Uncle Charlie asked when he returned home.

"Molasses cake," Corine answered. There were pans filled with cake all over the house. There was enough for everyone in Locust Bayou!

Corine didn't like to go fishing, but she often went to Johnson Lake with the family. Corine was afraid of the water. "When I went out in the boat, I shook so hard the boat rocked!"

Corine and her sister saw a lot of silent movies when they were growing up. Their father ordered the movies and showed them in his house. He hung a white sheet on the wall for a movie screen. People paid money to watch the black-and-white films.

Corine and her sister worked on their uncle's farm and for neighbors. Corine remembers long days when she pulled the cotton from the plants and put it in a rough cloth sack. The work made the ends of her fingers raw. When Corine was a teenager, she earned money by cleaning houses.

Work often kept the twins from school. When there was time, they walked two miles to a one-room schoolhouse.

Corine married Jack Bunn in 1926. They lived in Arkansas and Texas for twenty years before moving to California with their three children, Oma, Dean, and Evelyn.

Today Corine lives in Oakland with her daughter Evelyn. When she isn't telling stories about her growing-up years, she enjoys puzzles, walking, and music.

Name_____

Questions about *Corine Bunn &*
Growing-up Years

1. Why do you think so many people came to honor Corine on her ninetieth birthday?

_____

_____

2. Why did Corine and her sister live with their Uncle Charlie?

_____

_____

3. Name three states in which Corine has lived.

_____

4. Do you think Corine made the best decision after all the molasses spilled into the bowl? Explain your answer.

_____

_____

_____

5. How long had Corine lived in Oakland when she celebrated her ninetieth birthday?

_____

6. Corine liked living on the farm when she was growing up. Now she lives in the city. If you could choose where you lived, which would you choose—in the city or on a farm? Explain your answer.

_____

_____

Corine Bunn & Growing-up Years

Vocabulary

A. Write the number of each word from the story on the line in front of its meaning.

1. celebrated   _____ helped others without being paid

2. proclaimed   _____ a syrup made from sugarcane

3. honored   _____ squares sewn together to make a bedcover

4. memories   _____ made needlework by looping thread with a hooked needle

5. crocheted   _____ announced officially

6. volunteered   _____ thoughts about past events

7. descendants   _____ foods mixed together to make a dish

8. quilt   _____ groups of people living in an area or town

9. communities   _____ had a party for a special event

10. molasses   _____ the offspring of related people

11. ingredients   _____ showed respect for a person

B. Write sentences using words 2, 6, and 7 above.

1. _____

_____

2. _____

_____

3. _____

_____

Celebrating Diversity • EMC 798

Name_____

Corine Bunn & Growing-up Years
Comparing Yesterday and Today

Under the word *Then* you'll see information about Corine's life in the early 1900s. Under the word *Now* are lines for you to write about your life. The first section has been done for you.

Hot Water

Then | Corine's family put a tub of water on the wood stove in the morning to heat during the day. The hot water was used for washing and bathing in the evening.

Now | *We have a hot water heater that heats the water. We turn on the faucet*

when we want hot water.

Chores

Then | Corine warmed the cows' feet on cold winter days by building bonfires.
She held the milk pail when the cows were milked.
She picked cotton.
She cooked and helped with the housework.

Now | _____

_____

_____

_____

School

Then | Corine went to a one-room schoolhouse when she wasn't working.
She walked two miles to school.

Now | _____

_____

Earning Money

Then | Corine worked in other farmers' fields.
She cleaned houses.

Now | _____

_____

Name_____

Favorite Foods

Then | Corine liked molasses cake.

Now | _____

_____

Favorite Entertainment and Activities

Then | Corine watched black-and-white silent movies.
She liked to cook.

Now | _____

_____

Transportation

Then | Corine and her family walked.
They rode in a wagon pulled by horses.

Now | _____

_____

Clothing

Then | Corine's aunt made most of her clothing.
Sometimes clothing was ordered from the Sears catalog.

Now | _____

_____

Dislikes

Then | Corine didn't like water or riding in a boat.

Now | _____

_____

Mrs. Grill was saying, "…and we'll make our very own melting pot right here in our classroom." It was 11:45. History class was ending, and everyone was getting ready for lunch except for Tom. Tom was sitting perfectly still, deep in thought.

Mrs. Grill included everyone in her history lesson. She talked about the Native Americans who were here first. She talked about early European settlers. She talked about African slaves who came to this country against their will. She talked about recent arrivals from Mexico, the Philippines, and all the corners of the earth. She told her class that some people called America a "melting pot" because it is made up of so many varied and wonderful cultures.

Then Mrs. Grill said her class was a melting pot of its own. To demonstrate how they all meshed together to create one unique class, she asked her students to bring in things that represented their heritages. "If you have nothing at home that represents your heritage, draw a picture of something that does," she said. "If you do not know where your ancestors are from, then you can bring in an item or draw a picture of something from a culture that you admire."

Those last words were Tom's out, but he didn't want to take an out. He sullenly got up from his desk and walked to the cafeteria where he found Carlos. "Hi," Tom said without his usual enthusiasm.

"Hi," Carlos responded, "What's wrong, Tom?"

"Mrs. Grill's assignment," Tom replied. "I don't want to choose a culture I admire. I want to choose my own heritage. I want to know my own ancestors. I at least want to know my own parents."

Carlos had been adopted just like Tom, but Carlos knew who his parents were. His mother even visited once in awhile. His dad always sent birthday gifts. His grandparents had adopted Carlos when he was two years old. His parents were unable to care for Carlos, but they were not entirely out of the picture.

Tom had never known his biological parents. His adoptive parents were wonderful. Tom would not trade a day of his life for the life of any other person. Still, he couldn't help but wonder about his background.

"Tom," Carlos said, "I don't know anything about your ancestors, but I know about you. You are my best friend and you always will be. Here, have one of my grandma's famous sugar cookies." Tom took the cookie, but he didn't feel like eating it.

At the dinner table that evening, Tom asked his mom and dad about their backgrounds. They were both German. Tom's mother told him that he could take her favorite nutcracker to school for the melting pot.

Tom walked to his neighbor Jenny's house. Jenny said her family was from Jamaica. Jenny gave Tom a seashell. "Maybe this could go into your melting pot," she said. On his way back home, Tom ran into another neighbor. Four-year-old Kevin said he didn't know anything about his ancestors. "What does 'Aunt Sisters' mean, anyway?" he asked Tom.

"Never mind, kid," Tom replied as he walked off.

"Tom!" Kevin yelled after him. "Do you want one of my frogs?"

Tom thanked Kevin for the gift. He put the frog in his jacket pocket next to the sugar cookie and walked home.

That night Tom had a wonderful dream. The next morning he took a large smile and medium-size box with him onto the school bus. The box sat next to Tom's desk until history class began. Mrs. Grill asked for contributions to the melting pot, which was really a big kettle from the cafeteria. Children added drawings, knickknacks, keepsakes, and junk. Marcella even added a wedge of cheese that had been imported from France.

Tom and his box were the last to reach the melting pot. "Mrs. Grill," he said, "I am proud to be a melting pot all by myself. My kind friends have shared their heritages with me. I am made up of all the nice people I meet every day. I am glad to add myself to the melting pot of Room 403." Tom put his mother's nutcracker into the big kettle. Then he added Jenny's seashell. Next came Carlos's grandma's sugar cookie. Finally, Tom reached into his box and added to his class's melting pot one plump green frog! He was certain Mrs. Grill would agree that the last addition could be set free in the creek behind the school when the history lesson was complete.

Name_____

Questions about *Melting Pot*

1. Why was Tom not happy after the history lesson?

_____

_____

2. Why might Tom want to know about his heritage?

_____

_____

3. Carlos had been adopted too. How did he know about his heritage?

_____

_____

4. If students in Mrs. Grill's class did not know anything about their ancestors, what could they add to the class's melting pot?

_____

_____

5. Why is the United States sometimes called a "melting pot"?

_____

_____

6. What do you think Tom meant when he said that he was a melting pot all by himself?

_____

_____

_____

Name_____

Melting Pot
Vocabulary

A. Using your own words, define these phrases from the story.

1. *biological parents* _____

_____

2. *adoptive parents* _____

_____

3. *Tom's out* (paragraph 4) _____

_____

4. *out of the picture* (paragraph 7) _____

_____

5. *the last addition* (last sentence of story) _____

_____

B. Complete the sentences below using these words from the story.

ancestors	imported	enthusiasm	cultures

1. The fabric for my mother's dress was _____ to this country from Japan.

2. Many African _____ enjoy music featuring drums and rhythm instruments.

3. My _____ lived in Spain.

4. Marie played all sports with great joy and _____.

Melting Pot

My Own Melting Pot

In the story Tom says that he is made up of all the nice people he meets every day. The kettle below is your melting pot. Fill it up with drawings of the people, events, and things that have shaped your own life.

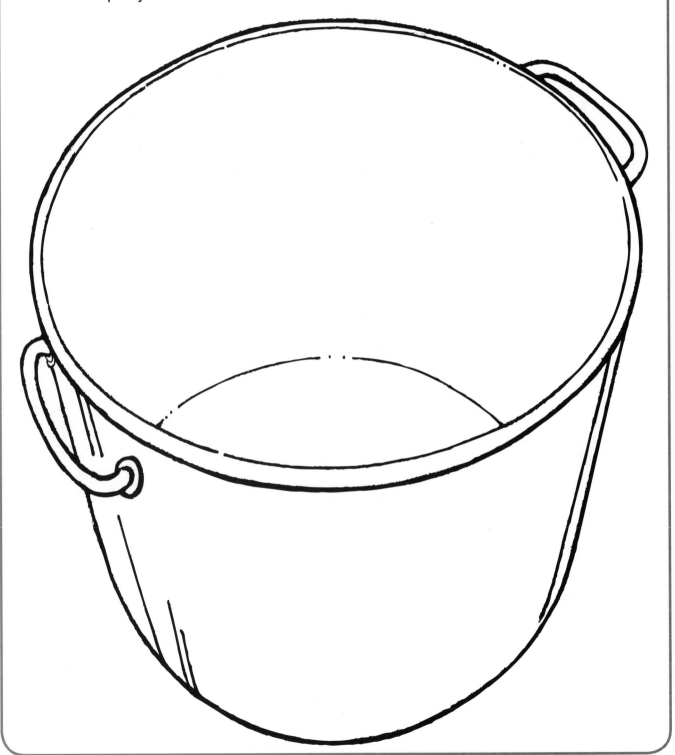

Melting Pot
A Wonderful Dream

Tom had a wonderful dream near the end of the story. When he awoke from his dream he knew what he was going to add to his class's melting pot. What might Tom have dreamed? Tell the story of Tom's dream.

Celebrating Diversity • EMC 798

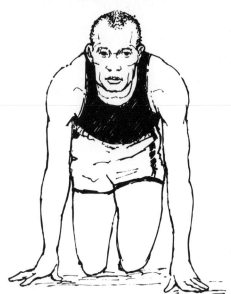

James Cleveland Owens was born on September 12, 1913. His seven brothers and sisters called him J. C. The family lived in Danville, Alabama. The whole family worked to earn enough to buy food for the family. J. C. picked cotton.

Hoping for a better life, the Owens family moved to Cleveland, Ohio. J. C. attended junior high and high school there. When J. C. entered school, the teacher asked his name. He answered, "J. C." The teacher misunderstood and wrote "Jesse." That name stayed with him the rest of his life.

At East Technical High School in Cleveland, Jesse was on the track team. He set or tied national and world records in track events. He studied and did well in school.

After he graduated he enrolled at Ohio State University. There he continued his winning ways on the track. Jesse didn't have a scholarship, so he had to work while he went to school. Despite the time taken by track and work, he was a good student.

When he was just a sophomore, his team went to a track meet in Michigan. He had decided to compete even though he had injured his back. In a 45-minute time period he did something amazing. He tied the world record for the 100-yard dash at 9.4 seconds. He broke the world running broad jump record with a 26 feet 8 1/2 inch jump. He finished the 220-yard hurdles in 22.6 seconds, another world record.

In 1936 Jesse Owens went to Berlin, Germany, to compete in the Olympics. The head of the German government was Adolph Hitler. He wanted to show the world what great athletes the Germans were. He spoke out against Jews and black people, saying they were inferior to Germans. Hitler was angry when Jesse Owens, the grandson of a slave, won four gold medals and broke world records during that Olympics. Other black members of the American team won more medals for the United States. They showed the world that they were outstanding athletes.

Hitler congratulated many medal winners, but he left the stadium to avoid congratulating Owens and the other black athletes. The German people cheered Owens and his outstanding performances even when Hitler was watching the games. One German athlete, Lutz Long, befriended Jesse in spite of Hitler. Lutz put his arm around Jesse after Jesse won the gold and he won the silver in the broad jump.

Jesse Owens was a hero after the 1936 Olympic Games. Even so, he faced discrimination in the United States when he returned home. He was not invited to the White House and he wasn't congratulated by the president. Jesse Owens, one of the world's greatest athletes, had to ride in the back of city buses. He couldn't live in many neighborhoods in the United States because he was black. Many restaurants refused to seat black people.

Owens decided to become a professional athlete. Despite hard work, his family had been poor all their lives. Now that he was famous he could earn money in professional meets and exhibitions.

People from all over the United States came to events to see the legendary Jesse Owens. Sometimes he was scheduled to race against animals and cars. He also toured with the Harlem Globetrotters' basketball team. At times when he didn't earn enough as an athlete, he worked as a janitor and a disk jockey.

By the time Jesse Owens was thirty-five years old, he had become a successful speaker and public relations person. He didn't need to compete in special events.

In his later years Jesse stopped running and jogging. He exercised by walking daily. He also lifted weights and swam to stay physically fit.

In 1976 he received the Medal of Freedom from President Gerald Ford. It is the highest honor an American can receive. He was finally recognized by the government for his achievements as an athlete and as a person. He died four years later.

1936 Olympic Triumphs

Jesse Owens ran the 100-meter dash in 10.3 seconds.

He completed the 200-meter dash in 20.7 seconds.

His running broad jump, a gigantic 26 feet and 5 3/8 inch leap, earned him another gold medal.

He was the lead member of the U.S. 400-meter relay team. The four American runners broke another world record with a 39.8 second time.

Jesse Owens earned a total of four gold medals during the games.

Name_____

Questions about *Jesse Owens*

1. How was J. C. Owens's name changed to *Jesse*?

   _____

2. Describe Jesse's accomplishments as a college athlete.

   _____

   _____

   _____

3. Why didn't Adolph Hitler congratulate winning black athletes at the Olympics?

   _____

   _____

   _____

4. In what ways were Owens and other black people discriminated against in the 1930s and 1940s?

   _____

   _____

   _____

5. Why do you think Jesse Owens was awarded the Medal of Freedom?

   _____

   _____

   _____

Name_____

Jesse Owens
Vocabulary

A. Complete the sentences below using words from the Word Box.

Word Box			
befriended	competed	discrimination	sophomore
relay	amateur	professional	

1. Jesse Owens _____ in the 100- and 200-meter dash, the broad jump,

   hurdles, and _____ races.

2. Owens broke several world records during his _____ year at
   Ohio State University.

3. Owens and other black people faced _____ in the United States.
   They couldn't eat or live in many places.

4. During the Olympic Games in Germany in 1936, Lutz Long, a German athlete,

   _____ Owens.

5. Owens, an _____ athlete before and during the Olympics, became a

   _____ athlete when he returned to the United States.

B. Write each word below on the line in front of its meaning.

   exhibitions   successful   recognized   dictator   legendary

1. _____ a ruler with power over the people

2. _____ gaining honor or wealth; achieving goals

3. _____ one who is admired and talked about for outstanding
   achievements; described as a hero

4. _____ singled out for special achievements; known

5. _____ special events and displays

Name_____

Jesse Owens
Write About It

Jesse Owens was a successful student, athlete, and speaker even though he faced many problems during his life. Write about the successes you would like to have during your life. Include what you think you would need to do to achieve your goals and be successful.

_____

_____

_____

_____

_____

_____

_____

_____

_____

_____

_____

_____

_____

_____

_____

Jesse Owens

Track Math

> 1 meter = 3.28 feet
>
> 1 meter = 1.09 yards

Use the information in the box, mental math, and your estimation skills to choose the best answer.

1. How many feet is the 100-meter race?

   a. 32 feet   b. 109 feet   c. 328 feet

2. How many yards is a 200-meter race?

   a. 656 yards   b. 218 yards   c. 3.09 yards

3. Which is longer, a 400-meter race or a 400-yard race? _____

4. A broad jump of 26 feet is about how many meters?

   a. 8 meters   b. 10 meters   c. 9 meters

5. How much longer did it take Jesse Owens to run the 200-meter dash than the 100-meter dash in the 1936 Olympics?

   a. 9.6 seconds   b. 31 seconds   c. 10.4 seconds

6. The U.S. 1936 Olympic 400-meter relay team set a world record by running the race in 39.8 seconds. How much under 40 seconds was their time?

   a. 2 seconds   b. 2 tenths of a second   c. 2 hundredths of a second

7. Is a 220-yard dash longer or shorter than a 200-meter dash? _____

One warm July Monday, thirteen-year-old Cheng Wan had a visitor. His father's business partner arrived from a small town in Montana. The business partner brought his ten-year-old son. While Cheng's father conducted business with his partner, Cheng gave young Danny a tour of his home, San Francisco's Chinatown. Here is Cheng's diary entry from the day he spent with Danny.

9:00 a.m.: Father introduced me to his business partner's son Danny. He asked me to show Danny around Chinatown while they conducted business. Danny looked nervous. He was about to spend an entire day with a stranger in a strange place. I had an idea. I marched Danny right to the Golden Gate Bakery. I bought two Chinese almond cookies for each of us. Danny smiled.

9:30 a.m.: Within half an hour, Danny's nervous look had been replaced with a look of curiosity. He wanted to know everything. Did I speak Chinese? Did I ever dance in a dragon costume during a Chinese New Year celebration? What did the owners of all the outdoor markets we were passing do when it rained? I told Danny I would ask one question. We stopped at a market that sold live fish and chickens and lots of fruits and vegetables. I spoke to the owner in Chinese. Danny was impressed. "What did he say? What did he say?" he asked.

"He said that when it rains he gets wet." We both laughed.

10:00 a.m.: Danny's curiosity turned to art. He liked the gilded storefronts and bold black lines of the symbols on business signs. We left Chinatown through the famous Dragon Gates on Grant Avenue and made our way to the Asian Art Museum in *dia fau*—the big city. There we saw all kinds of intricate woodcarvings, oriental jewelry, and Chinese watercolor paintings. Now Danny was ready for a history lesson.

11:00 a.m.: We made our way back to Chinatown's Chinese Culture Center. There we learned about the history of Chinatown. Danny found out that many Chinese left China in the 1840s because of a great famine and peasant rebellions. He was surprised so many decided to move halfway around the world to the United States.

The Chinese called America *Gum San,* or Golden Mountain. It was said to be full of gold and promise. "At first there were many jobs for the new immigrants," I told Danny as we walked to the old St. Mary's Church. The church was built by the hands of the early Chinese laborers who settled at Portsmouth Square, the heart of Chinatown. "The railroad tracks were laid by the Chinese too," I told Danny, "but when the economy turned bad, the jobs dried up."

I explained that some white settlers blamed the Chinese for taking their jobs away. Laws were passed that kept the Chinese from moving to the United States for a while. The Chinese who already lived here stuck together during the difficult years. Chinatown grew from a few blocks in size to a ten-block grid.

Then tragedy struck. In 1906 an earthquake shook San Francisco. Fires were ignited all over the city. By the time the fires ceased, Chinatown lay in ruins. It took many years to rebuild and repopulate the area between Broadway and Bush Streets and Kearney and Stockton Streets. "Today," I told Danny, "Chinatown is home to more than 10,000 Chinese residents."

12:30 p.m.: Danny enjoyed the history lesson. He marveled at the amount of work it must have taken to build the huge, gorgeous St. Mary's without modern tools. Thinking of all that work made Danny ready for some lunch. We walked on to the Bow Hon Restaurant. Danny wanted to have whatever I was going to have, so I ordered two of everything—po pos (boiled dumplings which I usually eat only on Chinese New Year), wonton soup, spring rolls, and kung pao prawns. Danny was disappointed when I told him not to eat his fortune cookie.

1:30 p.m.: Now Danny knew why I didn't let him eat his dessert! We stood in front of a fortune cookie factory. "They taste much better fresh from the factory," I told him. We took the whole tour. Then we ate six fortune cookies—each! Danny kept all of his fortunes in his pocket. I let him have mine too. Then I saw Danny eat the cookie he had saved from Bow Hon's. One of his fortunes must have said he would eat a lot today!

2:30 p.m.: Danny wanted to buy gifts for people at home, so we went shopping. At the Eastern Treasure Gift Shop he found a doll for his baby sister and some red silk slippers for his mother. At another shop he bought a wooden chess set for his best friend. He chose Chinese herbal teas for his grandmother.

4:00 p.m.: It was almost time for us to pick up some fresh fish for dinner. But we had to make one more stop. Danny couldn't leave until he had met my friends, Lim and Chin. We wandered over to Stockton Street to the Chinatown Neighborhood Center. As on all Monday afternoons, my two old friends were playing Bingo. Danny couldn't stop staring at the men's long white beards and wrinkled faces. He thought Lim and Chin must be a hundred years old! Neither one of them is older than eighty-five. They had a good laugh at a ten-year-old boy who couldn't stop staring at their beards! Danny laughed too, and we all had a wonderful visit. "Bingo!" Lim yelled, and we all cheered.

4:45 p.m.: I let Danny choose the fish for dinner from an open-air market on Grant Street. We picked out fruits and vegetables too, and even bought my mother some flowers. Danny wanted to make a good impression on my mother because he wants to visit us again. Next time he says he will stay for a week. "Next time," I said, "I hope you will invite me to visit Montana!"

Name_____

Questions about *Cheng Wan's Visitor*

1. Why might Danny have been nervous when he first arrived in Chinatown?

_____

_____

2. Where could Cheng and Danny have been found at 4:15 p.m.?

_____

3. Do you think Cheng's family eats much seafood? Explain your answer.

_____

_____

4. Do you think Danny and Cheng enjoyed their day together? How do you know?

_____

_____

_____

5. Tell about four things Danny learned during his day in Chinatown.

_____

_____

_____

6. Why might Cheng want to visit Montana?

_____

_____

Name_____

Cheng Wan's Visitor
Vocabulary

Complete the crossword puzzle using the words in the Word Box and the definitions below.

Across

2. a system of organizing production and distribution

4. people who move from one country to another

7. complex and delicate

10. good luck or destiny

12. workers

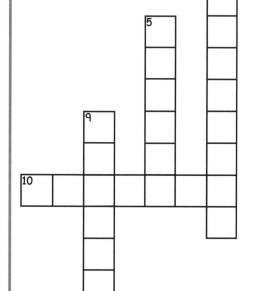

Down

1. a scarcity of food

3. to direct or manage, as in business

4. made a positive impression

5. Chinese for "big city"

6. covered in gold

8. an eagerness to learn

9. made with herbs

11. a low-paid farmer

Word Box

conduct (verb)	intricate
impressed	curiosity
gilded	laborers
economy	famine
peasant	dia fau
fortune	herbal
immigrants	

My Diary

Cheng Wan's Visitor

Dear Friends

Write a single letter addressed to both Danny and Cheng inviting them to come and visit you. Describe to them some of the things you will see and do while they are visiting.

_____

Dear Danny and Cheng,

_____

_____

_____

_____

_____

_____

_____

_____

Your friend,

_____

Name_____

Cheng Wan's Visitor
Around the U.S. in 90 Days

You are hosting a visitor from China. You have three months (and lots of money for airfare and fun) to show him just what America is all about. List below the places you will visit to give your friend a well-rounded taste of America. Explain what you will do at each stop and why the stop is important. A sample stop has been completed for you. Use another sheet of paper if you want to include more stops.

Los Angeles

I will take my visitor on a tour of Hollywood so he will know how important movies and television programs are to American entertainment. I will let him see the sights of Disneyland and ride the rides because it is a national treasure. I will let him swim in the ocean because coastlines are important geographical features in the United States.

Stop 1 _____

_____

_____

Stop 2 _____

_____

_____

Stop 3 _____

_____

_____

Stop 4 _____

_____

_____

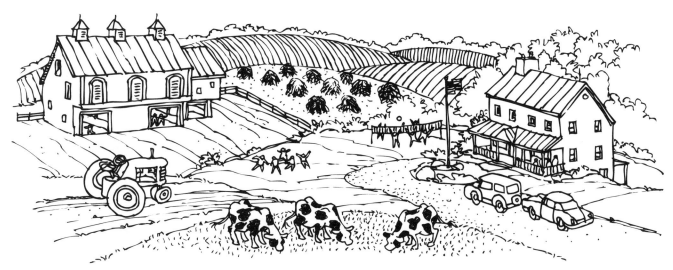

As a child, I adored summer Sunday afternoons. Precisely at twelve o'clock, church let out with the loud ringing of the huge bell. In a flash, my cousins and I burst out the nearest door and into each other's cars in a wild and disorderly fashion. We were off to Grandma and Grandpa's farmhouse!

The first order of business was to devour a large, loud, and long noontime meal. Then we slammed our way out Grandma's back door. The fun was about to begin. We chased barn cats, stomped in cow pies, and threw each other into haystacks. We explored every nook and cranny of Grandpa's old barn. Newest-addition cousins sat in a playpen beside the volleyball net where the adults gathered. Sometimes we snatched up our cousins so they could ride in wheelbarrows or kiss the cows. They learned the rules of kick-the-can and king-of-the-hill before they could speak.

On lucky Sunday afternoons, Grandpa would join us in the field behind the barn. We took turns riding on Old John Deere all around the farm. The cows mooed their complaints when we entered their domain. We just laughed and reached out to pet them on the nose. Sometimes we even did real work—planting seed or gathering eggs. The chickens hated Sundays as much as the cows did. Grandpa always assured them we were good and gentle helpers.

Eventually the sun began to set. The adults stopped their fast-paced volleyball game, groaning about bug bites, sore muscles, and hunger. Adults and kids alike clamored back into the mosquito-free house. Supper was a makeshift affair featuring dinner leftovers. The adults then retired to the living room, collapsing on couches and rocking chairs. We kids headed for the cellar to battle with cue-stick swords in between games of eight ball.

Sometimes I stayed upstairs. I silently found a corner on the floor of the adult world and listened. The talk was always of ethics. Is it ever okay to lie? Do all people have a conscience?

Never resolved, the issues were sooner or later shelved for further discussion. The men then moved their party to the cellar. When the door squeaked open at the top of the stairs, children left the pool table. It was our elders' turn to play.

For a while then, we explored the basement. There were flowers drying in the cramped quarters behind the massive furnace. There was a tall, rickety old metal box that Grandpa showered in after his shifts on the B&O railroad. There was a fruit cellar full of fresh-fruit bins. Vegetables Grandma had canned filled the tall shelves.

Eventually, one of us was caught forgetting to shut the fruit cellar door. Besides, we were making too much noise and bumping into cue sticks at crucial moments. Then we would all be booted upstairs.

Once there, the womenfolk offered us a choice. We could play outdoors or move into the "porch." The porch was a huge, fully enclosed room. In any self-respecting California ranch home, it would have been called the "recreation room."

Deciding our next move always turned into a debate for us kids. Firefly catching and midnight tag were the main outdoor attractions. Games involving the hundreds of buttons from Grandma's button box were an indoor option. We usually selected some mix of indoor and outdoor fun. As a result, the porch door slammed frequently and bugs were let into the house. The adults were quick to comment on both events.

Slowly, a few at a time, aunts and uncles surrendered to the threat of another Monday morning arriving too soon. Cousins were coaxed into cars with bribes of Grandma Ruth's cookies. Children's games fell apart, and adult talk slowed with each disappearing brood. My family was always the last to leave, and I was the most reluctant to say good-bye to another Indiana Sunday.

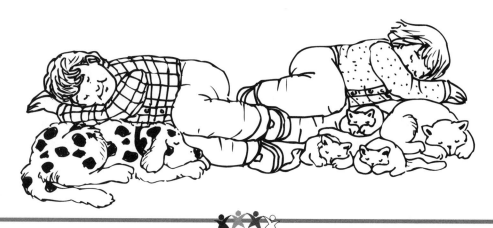

Questions about *Indiana Sundays*

1. The main purpose of this biographical narrative is to

   a. relate facts about farming techniques

   b. describe emotions and experiences the author had as a child

   c. persuade readers to live in the country

   d. paint a picture of an imaginary world

2. What is a "newest-addition cousin"?

   _____

3. Did the author enjoy her childhood visits to her grandparents' farm?
   Find two statements from the story to justify your answer.

   _____

   _____

   _____

4. What does the phrase *". . .aunts and uncles surrendered to the threat of another Monday morning arriving too soon"* mean?

   _____

   _____

5. Place the following events in *Indiana Sundays* in chronological order. The first one has been completed for you.

   _____ A large lunch is enjoyed by the family.

   _____ The sun begins to set and everyone moves indoors.

   _____ The men ask the children to leave the basement.

   __1__ Church ends and the entire family heads to the grandparents' farm.

   _____ Children play on the farm as the adults play volleyball.

   _____ Families begin to leave one by one.

   _____ Kids play games with Grandma's buttons.

Name_____

Indiana Sundays
Figurative Language

1. An **idiom** is an expression that does not mean exactly what the words say. For example, *break the news* has nothing to do with *breaking.* Find the idiom in the third sentence of paragraph 8 of the story and write it here. What does it mean?

_____

_____

2. Match the words used in Midwestern dialect in the story with their synonyms on the right.

dinner	lunch
porch	family
cellar	corner or small space
brood	basement
nook and cranny	women
womenfolk	recreation room

3. What piece of farm equipment is "Old John Deere"? _____

Word Meaning

Write the number of each word from the story on the line in front of its meaning.

1. makeshift   _____ extremely important

2. massive   _____ standards of right and wrong

3. ethics   _____ a substitute or temporary solution

4. crucial   _____ moved with great noise and confusion

5. disorderly   _____ surrounded on all sides; closed up

6. devour   _____ large and bulky

7. enclosed   _____ in an unruly manner

8. clamored   _____ withdrew from activity

9. retired   _____ to eat greedily

Name_____

Indiana Sundays
Personal Images

The author's thoughts are full with images and words that describe her feelings about summer Sunday afternoons spent at her grandparents' farm.

Fill the other thought bubble with words and images that describe your feelings about things your family does on Sundays. Make the head look like you.

Author

soft hay

itchy mosquito bites

laughter and running

Grandma's chewy cookies

smooth warm eggs

moist, velvety cow noses

feeling loved and secure

sticky peach juice on my face

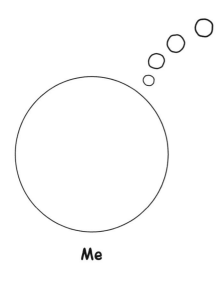

Me

115   Celebrating Diversity • EMC 798

Name_____

Indiana Sundays
Map Reading

Farms across the United States provide us with food. The map below shows some of the crops and animals that are raised in various states today. Use the map and its key to help you answer the questions below the map.

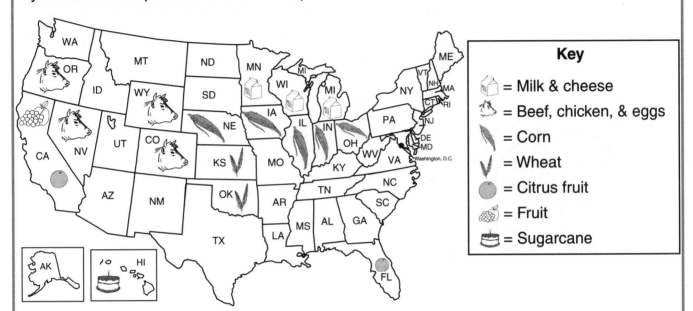

Key

= Milk & cheese

= Beef, chicken, & eggs

= Corn

= Wheat

= Citrus fruit

= Fruit

= Sugarcane

1. According to the map, what did Grandma and Grandpa likely grow on their farm?

_____

2. If you wanted steak and eggs for breakfast, in which four states could you get your whole meal fresh from the farm?

_____

3. Factories that make flour might buy the grain they need from which two states?

_____

4. Which state is this nation's primary sugarcane producer?

_____

5. Macaroni and cheese lovers might like to live in which three states?

_____

6. Many of the farms in these states could be called "orchards."

_____

Ballerina Maria Tallchief* inherited the proud bearing and grace of the Osage. She was born on an Indian reservation in Oklahoma in 1925. Her father, Alex Tall Chief, was a prominent member of the Osage tribe.

The Tall Chief family lived in an imposing brick house atop the highest hill in town. The Osage received a great deal of money because of oil found under their tribal land. The money was more than enough to support the family, so Alex Tall Chief never felt any need to go to college, nor to have a career.

Maria's no-nonsense mother came from Irish and Scottish ancestors. Her husband's lack of ambition troubled Ruth Tall Chief. She wanted her children to get more out of life. She also felt that music should be a part of her children's lives. Maria and her younger sister, Marjorie, began music and dance lessons around the age of three.

Maria and her sister showed great promise in both music and dance, even when quite young. Ruth wanted her girls to have careers on the stage. She felt they would have a better chance in Hollywood. So the family moved to Los Angeles, California, when Maria was starting second grade.

Maria knew she wanted to be a dancer or a musician. But which? Her mother believed she should be a concert pianist. Maria enjoyed music, but disliked the long hours of practicing alone. She liked to be with people.

The sisters began studying with a teacher named Bronislava Nijinska. Nijinska was well known in the world of dance. She was a famous ballerina in Russia before coming to the U.S.

Madame Nijinska was a wonderful but demanding teacher. She told Marjorie and Maria they had to start over. They had talent, she said, but they had learned everything wrong. She made Maria work harder than she had ever worked. She also helped Maria arrive at a decision. With encouragement from her teacher, Maria began to see herself as a ballerina.

*Maria was born Elizabeth Marie Tall Chief. She changed her first name to Maria. Then, as a teenager, she shortened her last name to one word, Tallchief.

Maria studied with Madame Nijinska for five years. Then, after high school, she was asked to tour with a professional ballet company. *Touring* means "going from city to city, dancing onstage."

Maria was seventeen. Her mother and father were concerned about her traveling without them. Also, Ruth Tall Chief still believed that Maria should become a concert pianist. Maria, however, was determined to dance. Finally they said she could accept the job.

This was an exciting new beginning for Maria Tallchief. She worked incredibly hard. After the tour she was asked to keep dancing for the company, which was called the Ballet Russe de Monte Carlo. She became one of the company's star ballerinas. It was during this time that she met George Balanchine.

Balanchine was a leader in American ballet. He was one of this country's most creative choreographers. A *choreographer* is someone who plans steps for dancers. Then he or she trains the dancers to do those steps. American ballet was not thought to be as beautiful as European and Russian ballet. Balanchine changed that. He created ballets that were original and exciting. He trained dancers to use their strengths. He showed Maria Tallchief how to become an even better dancer than she had been.

In 1946, when Maria was twenty-one years old, she married George Balanchine. He asked her to join his ballet company. The company later became the famed New York City Ballet. Maria danced there for many years, performing in as many as eight shows a week. The company became very popular.

So did Maria. She became the United States' first world-class prima ballerina, or ballet star. Around the world, people were awed by her. Newspapers called her "enchanting," "brilliant," and "electrifying."

In 1951 Maria's marriage to Balanchine ended. Still, she continued to dance with the New York City Ballet. She married again and had a daughter. In 1965 she finally retired from the New York City Ballet.

Maria was ready for new challenges. She worked with the Chicago Lyric Opera Ballet and briefly with the Hamburg Ballet. Then, in 1980, she started her own company, calling it the Chicago City Ballet. There she and her sister, Marjorie, taught young dancers to love the ballet.

Maria Tallchief was honored by her home state in 1953. She was given the name Wa-Xthe-Thomba. This means "Woman of Two Worlds." The name celebrates her achievements as a prima ballerina and as a Native American.

Questions about *Maria Tallchief*

1. Tell how each of the people listed below influenced Maria's life.

   Ruth Tall Chief

   _____

   _____

   Madame Nijinska

   _____

   _____

   George Balanchine

   _____

   _____

2. How would a career as a concert pianist have been different from that of a ballerina? In what ways might it have been similar?

   _____

   _____

   _____

   _____

   _____

3. Make a list of adjectives that describe Maria Tallchief.

   _____

   _____

   _____

Name_____

Maria Tallchief
Vocabulary

A. Use clues from the story to help you write definitions for each word or phrase below. Then write a sentence using each word or phrase.

1. choreographer: _____

_____

_____

2. prima ballerina: _____

_____

_____

3. imposing: _____

_____

_____

B. Use these words from the story to complete the sentences below.

determined   retired   original   strengths   electrifying

1. Jaime studied for two hours last night. He's _____ to get a good grade on the science test.

2. Keisha was so exciting in her role as Juliet! She gave an _____ performance.

3. We need _____ stories for the creative writing contest. Please don't imitate stories by other writers.

4. My grandmother _____ from her job last year. Now she and Granddad spend more time with us.

5. That runner's weakness is that she isn't a fast starter. Her _____ are that she is smart and she can run a long way without getting tired.

Name_____

Maria Tallchief

Making Choices

A. Maria had to make a choice between piano and ballet. It was a hard decision because she enjoyed both. Do you think she did the right thing? Tell why or why not.

_____

_____

_____

_____

B. All of us have to make choices at times; whether to play basketball or volleyball, or which friends to sit with at lunch. Think about a time when you had to make a hard decision. Use the T-chart to list the reasons for each choice.

Reasons to	Reasons to

C. On another sheet of paper, write a paragraph or more about the choice you made and how you came to your decision.

Maria Tallchief

Thinking About the Arts

Maria Tallchief was a gifted artist. Ballet falls into a group of art called **performing arts**. Other examples of performing arts include music, acting, and mime. Performing arts involve the artist doing something for an audience.

Painting is a **visual art**. Other examples of visual arts include sculpture, pottery-making, collage, and photography. Visual arts involve the artist making something for other people to look at.

1. What are some other examples of visual or performing arts?

_____

2. Which visual or performing arts do you enjoy? Tell what you like most about them.

_____

_____

_____

3. Would you rather be the audience or the artist? Why?

_____

_____

4. Give examples of artists you know about that are not listed above. These people don't have to be famous; they can be family members or friends. Describe the art form chosen by each artist.

_____

_____

_____

Helen Keller

In the year 1890, the town of Tuscumbia, Alabama, had a law about dogs. If one was found wandering around town without its owner, it would be put to death. Lioness, the dog of a famous girl who lived in Tuscumbia, roamed the streets alone one night. When Lioness was killed, people from Europe and all around the United States sent the dog's owner money. They wanted the famous little girl to buy a new dog. The famous little girl had other plans for the funds. The ten-year-old thanked people for their concerns. Then she asked to use the money to send Tommy Stringer, a poor blind boy, to a special school. Helen Keller's lifelong career of giving was off to an early start.

Three years earlier, Helen Keller would not have been able to offer this help. The seven-year-old was trapped inside a dark and quiet world. A fever she had as an infant had left her blind and deaf. She used simple signs to let her family know of her needs, but she did not understand language. She did not know why the people around her moved their lips. She did not know that things had names. The trouble she had communicating frustrated Helen. In anger she dashed fragile objects across the room, threw wild temper tantrums, and even locked her mother in the pantry.

Helen's parents knew they must do something about their wild child! They found Helen a tutor. Annie Sullivan had a challenge on her hands. First she "tamed" Helen by not giving in to her tantrums. Then she taught her all about language. Annie traced patterns on Helen's palm with her finger. At first Helen did not grasp that the patterns stood for words. But when she began to understand, there was no stopping Helen. She learned so quickly that she became famous worldwide for her accomplishments. She mastered not only English, but also French, German, Greek, and Latin. She later wrote that language freed her. Helen would spend the rest of her life freeing others with her words.

Annie stayed with Helen for fifty years. She took Helen on long walks, quiet picnics, and zooming toboggan rides. She spelled in Helen's hand and translated countless books into Braille for Helen to read. By 1905 Helen had graduated from college with honors, written a book about her life, and learned to speak. Upon graduation, Helen became a member of the Massachusetts Commission for the Blind.

Annie and Helen next hit the road. They were invited to Washington, D.C., Europe, and Japan. At each stop they shook hands with presidents, prime ministers, kings, and princes. Most importantly, they spoke to crowds of people. Helen gave other disabled people hope by speaking of the independence she now experienced. Sometimes she spoke of the unfair treatment of women, the poor, and others who struggled for justice. Always, Helen Keller asked her audiences to treat themselves and all other people with dignity and respect.

When Annie Sullivan died in 1936, Helen missed her dearly. She began a book about Annie. When her notes were destroyed in a house fire, she began a new book. In 1955 *Teacher* was published.

Helen lived 32 years after Annie died. With the help of a new assistant, Polly Thomson, she continued to spread hope around the globe. When soldiers in World War II were blinded in battle, Helen visited them in the hospital. When the American Foundation for the Blind was formed, Helen and Polly raised funds for the organization. They visited Scotland and Ireland, South Africa, and the Middle East. They spoke to crowds and supported laws that helped the disabled and disadvantaged.

In 1960 Helen's friend and companion Polly Thomson died. Helen was old and fragile herself by then. She suffered a series of strokes and was seldom seen in public during the next eight years. In 1968 Helen Keller died. At the time of her death she had written four books and worked for several foundations for the blind. She had given speeches and visited the disabled around the world. She had been the subject of three movies. Her lifelong determination to succeed and her concern that all others have the chance to live a full life earned Helen Keller the title "America's First Lady of Courage."

Questions about *Helen Keller*

1. Do you think the people who gave young Helen Keller money to buy a new dog were upset when she wanted to spend the money on something else? Why or why not?

_____

_____

_____

2. When Helen was a young girl, why did it seem unlikely she would grow into a woman who would help other people?

_____

_____

_____

3. Why did Helen Keller become known as "America's First Lady of Courage"?

_____

_____

4. Why do you think Helen wanted to write a book about Annie Sullivan?

_____

_____

5. Helen could not do two things that most people can do easily—see and hear. Still, she could do some very remarkable things. List things Helen did in her lifetime that many people will never do.

_____

_____

_____

Name_____

Helen Keller
Root Words

The **root word** (base word) is the main part of a word before prefixes or suffixes are added. Write the root words of these words from the story.

1. countless _____

2. wandering _____

3. graduation _____

4. determination _____

5. frustrated _____

6. communicating _____

7. accomplishments _____

8. organization _____

9. disadvantaged _____

10. assistant _____

Writing Sentences

Use each of these words from the story in a sentence of your own.

destroyed   tantrum   career   fragile

1. _____

_____

2. _____

_____

3. _____

_____

4. _____

_____

Helen Keller

Helen Keller and Me

1. When Helen Keller was a young girl, she felt very frustrated at not being able to communicate with others. Tell about a time you felt very frustrated. How did you deal with your frustrations?

_____

_____

_____

_____

2. Helen Keller accomplished a lot more in her lifetime than many people expected of a deaf and blind girl. Tell about a time you surprised yourself or someone else by accomplishing something great.

_____

_____

_____

_____

3. Helen Keller's personal philosophy was "Faith is the strength by which a shattered world shall emerge into the light." Write a one-sentence philosophy that tells what you think life is all about.

_____

_____

_____

_____

Name_____

Helen Keller
Symbolic Actions

Before Helen Keller understood language, she used simple actions to communicate. She pretended to slice and butter a piece of bread when she wanted to eat. She imitated putting on reading glasses when she wanted her father. If you had to use actions to communicate the following information, what actions would you choose? The first one has been done for you as an example.

1. You are outside and want to go inside. __Imitate knocking on a door._____

2. You want to go for a drive. _____

3. You want to read a book. _____

4. You want to listen to music. _____

5. You want to watch a movie. _____

6. You want to visit a friend. _____

7. You want to play basketball. _____

8. You want to go shopping. _____

9. You want to go to school. _____

10. You want a drink. _____

                                       Celebrating Diversity • EMC 798

On April 9, 1865, the American Civil War ended. During the next five years the Congress of the United States passed three constitutional amendments in an effort to undo the injustices of the past. The Thirteenth Amendment abolished slavery. The Fourteenth Amendment made former slaves citizens of the United States. The Fifteenth Amendment gave these new citizens the right to vote. In 1875 the Civil Rights Act outlawed discrimination in public places. The shameful story of America's mistreatment of African Americans *seemed* to be in its final chapter. Unfortunately, it was not.

In 1883 the Supreme Court invalidated the Civil Rights Act of 1875. African-American citizens could now be legally barred from "white establishments." Southern states found ways around the mandates of the Fifteenth Amendment. Black men's jobs and lives were threatened if they chose to register to vote.

Nearly one hundred years after the Civil War, Martin Luther King, Jr., stood in the city of Montgomery and mourned the lack of progress the nation had made in assuring the civil rights of all citizens.

Martin Luther King, Jr., was born to an Alabama minister and his wife in 1929. Although his childhood was pretty typical overall, Martin did endure injustices because of the color of his skin. He could not go to "white" schools or drink out of "white" drinking fountains. One day his white neighbors asked Martin to stop playing with their son. Once, when Martin was shopping with his mother, a white woman struck him on the cheek and called him a bad name. On another shopping trip, a shoe salesman refused service to Martin's father. His father had refused to sit in the "black section."

Martin Luther King, Jr., had cause to be angry. Yet Martin didn't think anger would solve the problems of injustice. He thought the answers could be found in love.

When Martin had finished his schooling, he became the pastor of a church in Montgomery, Alabama. He had enjoyed comfortable freedoms in the northern colleges he had attended. Now he felt called to help the people in the South experience those same freedoms.

Just how Martin could change things in the South was not clear. Then, in December of 1955, he saw a possible path. On December 1 an African-American woman named Rosa Parks was arrested for refusing to give up her bus seat to a white passenger. Mistreatment of blacks on Montgomery city buses was common. Drivers called them bad names. They drove away from bus stops before black passengers could board. More than once, black citizens were arrested when they refused to offer their seats to white people.

This time something was different. Rosa Parks called the National Association for the Advancement of Colored People and asked for help. Ms. Park's case would go to court. News of the case spread quickly in the city of Montgomery. People gathered at Martin's church and formed a plan.

Montgomery blacks would refuse to ride the bus that Monday. They would take cars or taxis to work. Or they would walk. Or they would stay home. Thousands of flyers were printed and passed out. The boycott worked! The buses in Montgomery were nearly empty on the morning of December 5, 1955.

Black leaders decided to continue the boycott until blacks were treated fairly on the buses. They elected Martin president of the group that would oversee the plan. The boycott lasted an entire year. At last, on December 20, 1956, the buses of Montgomery, Alabama, became integrated. Martin Luther King, Jr., was no longer a single individual who felt a calling to right wrongs. He was now the leader of a massive movement for civil rights.

Montgomery was just the beginning. Next, Martin became president of an organization called the Southern Christian Leadership Conference. This organization asked people of all colors and walks of life to break unjust laws. To oppose laws forcing blacks to sit in the back of buses, Freedom Riders rode buses all over the South. They would sit anywhere they liked. Sit-ins were held. This was where blacks sat in seats reserved for whites at restaurants and theaters. Black citizens conducted kneel-ins at "white" churches. Martin Luther King, Jr., was uniting hundreds of thousands of people in a struggle for justice. His eloquent speeches, remarkable courage, and insistence on peace brought people of all races together.

Martin next organized marches to show government officials that people were ready to outlaw segregation. Hundreds of thousands of people joined Martin's marches. His August 28, 1963, March on Washington drew a crowd of 250,000. In front of the Lincoln Memorial, many famous people spoke about the need for civil rights. Martin Luther King, Jr., was the day's final speaker. His "I Have a Dream" speech expressed hope for a day when people of all races would live in harmony. The speech was met with thunderous applause and continues to be quoted around the world today.

Finally, on July 2, 1964, the United States Congress passed another Civil Rights Act. This one would not be dismissed by the Supreme Court. Martin Luther King, Jr., earned the Nobel Prize for Peace that year. He had proven that nonviolent reform was possible.

It was not always easy for Martin to persuade his followers or himself that injustices must be repaid with love. Martin and his family received hundreds of threatening phone calls. His house was bombed. His brother's house was bombed. Fellow pastors' houses were bombed. Churches were bombed. Southern states used old laws to arrest thousands of protesters. Marchers were attacked by police dogs and blasted by fire hoses. People were injured, and people were killed. Some black leaders wanted to fight violence with violence. Martin stood behind his belief in the power of love.

Still, it was a bullet that killed Martin on April 4, 1968. The man who refused to turn to hate or anger was killed by violence. Yet his dream lives on. Citizens of the whole world continue to work toward a day when all people can live in peace and civil justice. Martin Luther King, Jr., can be thanked for defining the dream.

Name_____

Questions about *We Shall Overcome*

1. "We Shall Overcome" was the theme song of the civil rights movement. Why do you think this song was chosen?

_____

_____

2. Why do you think Martin Luther King, Jr., chose to effect change through love rather than through anger and hate?

_____

_____

3. Martin was killed before he could put his latest idea into action. His latest idea was to work for the rights of poor Americans of all races. Do you think we would have less poverty in the United States today if Martin had lived longer? Why or why not?

_____

_____

_____

4. Martin was arrested many times during his lifetime for civil disobedience. Why do you think he chose to do things that would result in his going to jail?

_____

_____

_____

5. Would you ever engage in civil disobedience? Why or why not?

_____

_____

_____

Name_____

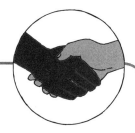

We Shall Overcome
Vocabulary

Read the definitions of these words from the story. Then select the correct word to complete each sentence below.

abolish	to get rid of
crusaders	people who work for reform
prohibited	legally not allowed
discrimination	the unfair treatment experienced by members of a group
civil rights	the rights or liberties of the citizens of a nation
civil disobedience	refusal to obey the laws or demands of government as a means of changing those laws
boycott	to have no dealings with a product or business
movement	an organized effort to bring about change

1. Do you think the civil rights _____ would have succeeded without Martin Luther King, Jr.?

2. Suffragettes were _____ for women's voting rights.

3. If we all _____ that gas station, perhaps they will lower their prices.

4. Tough laws are needed to _____ the pollution of our lakes and rivers.

5. The sign says that fishing in this stream is _____.

6. Police officers must not abuse the _____ of those they arrest.

7. Businesses that engage in _____ in hiring can be taken to court.

8. In some nondemocratic countries, the government does not tolerate

_____.

Name_____

We Shall Overcome

Judge Me by My Character

Martin Luther King, Jr.'s, dream was that one day people would be judged by their character rather than by their skin color.

How is Martin's character described in the story? Complete the character map below by writing facts from the story that support each of the headings.

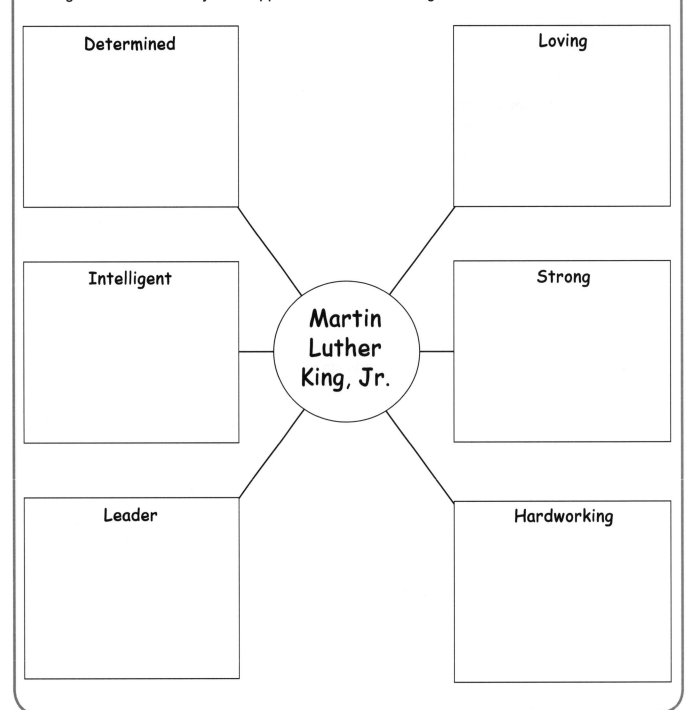

Determined

Loving

Intelligent

Strong

Martin Luther King, Jr.

Leader

Hardworking

The Civil War had been over for two months. President Abraham Lincoln had signed the Emancipation Proclamation two and a half years earlier. Slavery was supposed to have ended, but word traveled slowly. On June 19, 1865, the blacks of Galveston, Texas, were still slaves.

Then, at a big house called Ashton Villa, Union army Major Gordon Granger read a paper called "General Order #3" to the people of Galveston. The order read:

General Order #3

The people of Texas are informed that, in accordance with a proclamation from the Executive of the United States, all slaves are free. This involves an absolute equality of personal rights and rights of property between former masters and slaves, and the connection heretofore existing between them becomes that between employer and hired labor. The freedmen are advised to remain quietly at their present homes and work for wages. They are informed that they will not be allowed to collect at military posts and that they will not be supported in idleness either there or elsewhere.

Many people didn't understand all the words in General Order #3. But four words were understood by all: *all slaves are free!*

It was as if Galveston had been turned upside down. People burst into joyful freedom songs. One person would start the song and others would make up verses. Milk buckets were left half-filled as former slaves walked (or ran) away. People leapt and laughed, ate and danced, prayed and sang. Some gathered to assure each other, yes, it was true. They were free! All over Galveston, former slaves celebrated freedom that day.

People today still choose June 19th as a day to celebrate freedom. In the beginning, "Juneteenth" celebrations were held mainly in Galveston and areas nearby. Then these people moved away from Texas, spreading across the United States and the world. Juneteenth spread too. Americans in other countries remember the holiday. In places as far away as Japan and Spain, Juneteenth is honored with speeches, festivals, and prayer.

There are lots of stories about how "June 19th" was shortened to *Juneteenth.* Most of these stories involve a little girl who was unable to say *nineteenth.* No one is really sure what the real story is.

For many Americans Juneteenth is a favorite holiday. In cities like Houston, Texas, and San Jose, California, events begin days or weeks earlier. Then, on the morning of June 19th, parades start up with the whine of fire engines and the music of marching bands. The day is packed with prayer services, picnics, games, and concerts. There are heaping tables of food, especially barbecue and red soda pop. These are old Juneteenth favorites. There may also be speeches, plays, poetry readings, and sporting events.

There have been years when people were not very interested in Juneteenth. This happened during World War II, probably because most people were thinking about the war. There have been times when African Americans faced so much racial prejudice that it seemed there was little to celebrate. But Juneteenth *is* still celebrated, because freedom demands a celebration.

Name_____

Questions about *Freedom Celebration*

1. Why was General Order #3 important?

_____

_____

2. How did the former slaves of Galveston react when they heard the reading of General Order #3?

_____

_____

3. Where were the first Juneteenth celebrations held?

_____

_____

4. How did the tradition of celebrating Juneteenth spread?

_____

_____

5. Describe three ways that people celebrate Juneteenth today.

_____

_____

_____

6. What do you think the author meant by the words *freedom demands celebration*?

_____

_____

Freedom Celebration
Vocabulary

A. The words below are formed from the root word *celebrate*. Use these words to complete the sentences.

celebration   celebrating   celebrated   celebrants   celebrity

1. Andrew is _____ the team's big win with a pizza party.

2. The famous author, Michael Nguyen, is visiting our library tomorrow. Everyone is excited about meeting such a big _____.

3. The town of Pine Grove holds a big _____ every year on Juneteenth.

4. The _____, people involved in the celebration, will line the street to watch the parade.

5. Lynn and Claudia are going to an art gallery to meet the _____ artist, Maya Soto.

B. Write definitions for the words below as they are used in the sentences above. You may use a dictionary if you need to.

1. celebration _____

_____

2. celebrating _____

_____

3. celebrants _____

_____

4. celebrated _____

_____

5. celebrity _____

_____

Answer Key

Note: Open-ended activity pages are not listed in this answer key.

Page 7
1. The dog jerked back and growled because he had a toothache, and Abuelita inadvertently hurt him.
2. We know that the story is set on the Gulf of Mexico, because Abuelita stares across the gulf toward her homeland. We also know that this is not an extremely rural area, because the two houses are very close together. We know from the language that the story is set in modern times.
3. Abuelita doesn't trust Mrs. Bass because Mrs. Bass doesn't speak much Spanish. Some students may also understand that Abuelita finds it hard to trust Mrs. Bass because cultural differences make her seem strange.
4. Mrs. Bass is deeply fond of General, and depends on him for companionship. She showed concern when General would not eat. She was fearful that he had a grave illness, and was extremely relieved to learn that he may only have a toothache.
5. David's grandmother is lonely and burdened with cultural prejudice. She is also kind, and eventually, understanding.
6. When Mrs. Bass thanked Abuelita for finding out what was wrong with General, Abuelita spoke to Mrs. Bass in English, saying, "You are welcome."
7. Most students will predict that Mrs. Bass will take General to the vet and that she and Abuelita will become friends. Some may predict that Abuelita will overcome her negative feelings toward English-speaking people and make other friends. Accept any well-reasoned response.

Page 8
A. 1. tramped, stomped, thudded
2. shook, bounced, clattered
3. gazed, looked
4. pulled, yanked
5. section, length
6. shrill, high-pitched
7. bashfully, carefully, timidly
8. weepy, teary
B. 1. creo que sí
2. Abuelita
3. gracias
4. sí

Page 10
1. Texas, Louisiana, Mississippi, Alabama, Florida
2. Texas
3. north
4. Galveston, Biloxi, Pensacola
5. Florida
6. Mississippi River, Rio Grande

Page 13
1. The president wrote a letter to apologize and send money to Japanese Americans who were forced to go to detention camps during World War II.
2. They were sent to detention camps. Americans thought the Japanese Americans would be loyal to Japan. They were afraid the Japanese Americans might spy or work against the United States.
3. It was land guarded by soldiers and surrounded with barbed wire. The family lived in one room. There was a dining room for everyone and a building for showers.
4. People moved to the farm while the family was in the detention camp. They had legal papers made up that said the farm was theirs.
5. He wants to save it for Sam's education. He said that everything except what you learn can be taken away from you. He wants Sam to have something valuable that he can always use.

Page 14

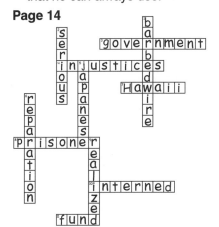

Page 16
Hawaii
California
discriminated
illegal
immigrants
citizens
law
internment
detention

Page 19
1. They planned to operate a medical clinic there.
2. Her parents and her brother were going. Also, she felt it was what God wanted her to do.
3. She was afraid Tamara might see how different the two of them were and not want to be her friend anymore. Some responses may quote the story, saying that Christine didn't want her friend to stare at her in five years and think, "How could I ever have been friends with this weird religious kid?"
4. She needed to know that Tamara knew they were different and liked her anyway.
5. The story is told from Christine's point of view. We know this because only Christine's thoughts and feelings are revealed. The author tells us she was exasperated. We are privy to her thoughts in paragraphs 3, 4, 6, 9, 13, and 15. Responses may include any of these examples.
6. The story is entitled *Girl Missionary* because Christine was both a missionary and a girl. Some responses may describe that the conflict in the story emerged from this fact. As a girl, she enjoyed her friendship with Tamara. As a missionary, she found huge obstacles in the way of that friendship—the five-year absence and the differences in their lifestyles.

Page 20
1. bleak
2. obvious
3. selfishly
4. eye contact
5. missionary
6. necessarily
7. assured
8. dramatic
9. considered
10. exasperated

Page 22
1. one month; the month of September; 30 days
2. one day
3. 6 days

Page 24
1. Most students will understand that the poem is set in a noisy place. Clues include the phrase "First-day chatter" in the left-hand verse and "Strange Sounds!" in the verse on the right.
2. The poem's title is a broad clue. Students should infer that the poem is set on the first day of

school and that the setting is crowded with people probably all talking at once. Some, drawing on personal experiences, may describe an air of excitement. A few students may conclude that the second character's perception of the setting could be different, even scary.

3. There are two main characters.

4. Students may conclude that this character is sensitive or friendly, because she smiles at the other character. A few students may also point out that this character seems more comfortable with the "first-day chatter" that "floats in the air." This line suggests that she finds the surroundings to be nonthreatening.

5. The character seems agitated, possibly afraid or even panicky. This is suggested by the line "Strange people! Strange sounds!" Some students may point out that the exclamation points suggest extremely strong feelings.

6. The other character smiles, a gesture that is understood across cultures.

7. The fact that she describes the chatter as "sounds" implies that things going on around her are unfamiliar. Students should understand that an unfamiliar language might seem like "strange sounds." The people might look strange because of cultural differences as well.

Page 25
Sentences for each item will vary.
1. drifts   3. beamed
2. peculiar
Possible choices include:
1. confusion, talk, noise, excitement, activity, conversation
2. bewildered, alone, friendly, confident, relaxed, quizzical
3. wave, grin, handshake, wink, nod

Page 27
A. Answers will vary, but could include other languages or other greetings in English such as "How do you do?, Hi, Howdy, What's happenin'?, What's up?, Yo," etc.
B. 1. Kwe   4. hello
2. hallo   5. Óla
3. Konnichi wa

Page 32
1. Clark and Daniel found the box in the attic of their grandfather's house. In the box was a V-letter and a pair of shoes Grandpa had owned as a child.

2. Grandpa hid the box in the attic in 1945 because he was angry that he had outgrown his leather shoes and had to give them to his younger brother. To make matters worse, he was expected to wear a pair of shoes he didn't like.

3. Clark had outgrown a pair of his favorite shoes and was unhappy about it. Grandpa wanted Clark to know that the same thing had happened to him when he was a child. Some students may point out that Grandpa wanted Clark to feel better about his situation.

4. Students will probably point out that there was no television. The family gathered around to listen to the radio. Favorite shows were mysteries, news reports, and comedians. On Saturday nights the family went to another family's house to play dominoes. While the adults played inside, the children played outside.

5. World War II was happening. Most of the country's resources were being used to produce what the soldiers needed to fight the war.

6. Students should infer that Grandpa felt guilty about what he had done. Clues include his comment, "It was pure meanness," and the author's description of him shaking his head as he talked to his grandsons about it.

Page 33
A. Possible answers include:
1. huge, large, enormous, gigantic, mammoth, massive, gargantuan, giant, elephantine, vast, colossal
2. tiny, small, wee, miniscule, petite, minute, undersized, teeny, teensy, itty-bitty
B. 1. comedian   4. astounded
2. dominoes   5. mused
3. wedged

Page 35
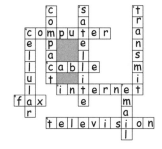

Page 38
1. The potato crop had failed and life in Ireland was difficult. She thought they would have a better life in Boston with their uncle.

2. There were rats that tried to eat the food. Passengers had to take all their food for the voyage with them. People were seasick and some had the fever. Some people died. The air was bad. The beds were boards stacked like shelves in a cupboard. People were crowded together.

3. He had disappeared.

4. Nicholas was a kind and generous person. He paid James's bill and arranged for his belongings to be sent to him to keep them safe. He took in the children and made them feel welcome.

5. Paul would help with horses and work in the garden. Bridget would clean.

6. Answers will vary.

Page 39
A. 1. immigrants   3. immigrant
2. immigrate   4. immigration
B. 1. official
2. due
3. passengers, voyage
4. passage
5. belongings, provisions, deck
6. dock

Page 45
1. He was a slave-catcher looking for runaways. Quakers often hid runaways.

2. If the runaway slaves came to his house, they could be caught and returned.

3. She cried and stood between the men and the wagon.

4. They all drove wagons to town to confuse the slave-catchers.

5. He used words that were a code— "This is the road."

6. Answers will vary. Possible answers: Rebecca knew what Jebediah was doing. The Friends worked together to help the slaves. They were a part of the Underground Railroad. Jebediah had a cart with a hidden compartment.

Page 46

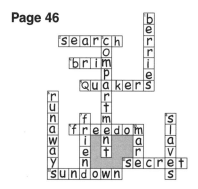

Page 48
1. station, escaped
2. Quakers
3. Slave-catchers, slave holders
4. conductors
5. runaways
6. northern states, Canada
7. slave-catchers, rewards (money)
8. Underground Railroad, secret route

Page 51
1. to learn English
2. She would have to help her with her homework. She wouldn't have time to visit friends and watch TV. She couldn't be in the play.
3. Lisa convinced her mother that Elena should be in the play. It would help her learn about holidays and improve her English.
4. They cleaned up the cemetery, decorated it with flowers, and put out food at home and at the cemetery to welcome the spirits of the dead. They set up a home altar with pictures and candles.
5. Answers will vary, but may mention that people want to remember those who they loved and who were important in their lives. Memorial Day is celebrated in the U.S., commemorating the lives of those who died defending our country.

Page 52
1. opened	4. agrees	7. long
2. forget	5. friends	8. ends
3. strange	6. together	9. after

1. soul	5. rehearsals
2. cemetery	6. celebrate
3. holiday	7. altar
4. cabinet	8. arrange

Page 53
The Day of the Dead
pan de muertos	marigolds
pictures	ancestors
altar	

Both Holidays
end of October	cemetery
skulls	spirits
skeletons	candles
candy	

Halloween
costumes	parties
trick-or-treating	

Page 54
A. 1. have finished
   2. had told
   3. had missed
   4. will celebrate
   5. will bring

B. 1. I'll bring pizza.
   2. You've done a good job.
   3. I've finished my homework.
   4. He'll be home soon.

Page 57
A. Grandma—moved to America from France, has a grandchild, still thinks of Leah
   Leah—Jewish, taken to concentration camp, brown hair, big brown eyes
   narrator—sensitive, concerned, intuitive
B. No, no one knows the answer to her questions. She was simply expressing herself.

Page 58
genocidal—deliberately exterminating a race of people
Aryan—in Nazi Germany—of European race, blond, blue eyed, non-Jewish
suspended—stopped
synagogues—a building for public Jewish worship
curfews—a signal or time after which people must remain inside until the next day
simultaneously—at the same time

Page 59
A. 1. relaxed, calm, happy
   2. sad, hesitant, puzzled, upset
   3. reminiscent, lonely, sad
B. Grandma's hesitancy, tears, hand-squeezes; darkening sky; narrator's concern

Page 63
1. She was eleven years old.
2. This event proved she could play as well as he could. It marked an important step in her progress as a golfer. It was important to Domingo because, as her loving father and coach, he shared in her successes.
3. Her school had no girls' golf team. They didn't want to allow a girl to play on the boys' team, but with the help of an attorney, Nancy persuaded them. The local country club didn't want to sponsor Nancy because she was Mexican American, but a club in Albuquerque was glad to do it.
4. She was sad and distracted. She may have been thinking that her mother would have wanted her to win, and was trying too hard.
5. She works hard. We know this because she practiced every day. She is not afraid of a challenge. At the age of twelve she competed and won in a statewide tournament. When the school said she couldn't play, she went back and tried again to persuade them, and did. Family is important to her. When she lost her mom, her game suffered. She didn't give up easily.
6. The author wanted the reader to understand that family is an important part of Nancy Lopez's life.

Page 64
Sentences for each item will vary.
A. 1. leading
   2. amateur
   3. failures
   4. unskilled
B. 1. competitors
   2. competition
   3. competitive
   4. competed

Page 66
1. address	5. rough
2. caddie	6. green
3. putter	7. tee
4. gallery	8. hole

3, 5, 8, 4, 2, 7, 1, 6

Page 69
1. Laurence's parents showed that reading and books were important. They read to their children and had the children read to them. Mr. Yep built a sandbox that helped to stimulate Laurence's imagination.
2. His family did not live near other Chinese American families. He did not speak Chinese as well as other Chinese Americans his age.
3. Laurence liked science fiction. He felt he had something in common with characters who found themselves in strange worlds. That was how he felt about being Chinese and American.
4. When Laurence was growing up, he felt he didn't belong to either the Chinese or the American cultures. Many of his books have characters that have to adjust to new places and different customs.

5. He did not do well in journalism classes. A teacher suggested that he was better at writing fiction than reporting.

Page 70
1. editor
2. grocer
3. philosopher
4. participant
5. citizen
6. spectator
7. student
8. teacher
9. author
10. parent
11. journalist

Page 75
1. The story game is a conversational game in which a young girl and her great-grandmother take turns telling about childhood happenings during their eras.
2. The old woman saw cars take the place of horses and buggies and washing machines take the place of washboards. Local, low-tech music concerts were replaced by high-tech, highly populated concerts. Indoor plumbing replaced outhouses, electric refrigerators replaced iceboxes, and children's chores were reduced from necessary field- and housework to casual gardening and light housework.
3. The great-grandmother helped her father farm and chop wood and her mother sew, cook, and do laundry. The girl helped her mother garden, wash clothes, and bake cookies.
4. The girl in the story probably anticipated completing a project with her grandmother because it is stated that the story game always ends with the completion of a project.

Page 76
A. 1. magnificently, extraordinarily
   2. containing a high amount of water vapor
   3. very great in size
   4. supplied with the necessary materials for an undertaking
   5. a gaseous element occurring in small amounts in the earth's atmosphere used chiefly in tubular electrical lamps
   6. rising or rolling in great swells or surges
   7. indisputably, certainly
   8. to force inhaled air through a liquid held in the back of the mouth
   9. relating to or containing herbs

B. 1. A washboard is a wooden or metal corrugated board on which clothes are rubbed in the process of laundering.
   2. "Privy" is a slang word for *outhouse,* which is a toilet housed in a small wooden building outside.

Page 81
1. A powwow gathers together many Native Americans in pride and celebration. Crafts, dances, songs, and food of the Native American culture are shared.
2. Powwows are organized in celebration of a special event such as the birth of a child, a good harvest, or just in celebration of life.
3. The Drum is an actual drum and also singers and dancers. The Drum is important to a powwow because it orchestrates all of the songs and dances that are performed.
4. Native American art probably incorporates so many symbols from nature because the lives of Native Americans before the arrival of Europeans were closely linked to nature. Things from nature provided people with food, shelter, and recreation. Ancient Native American religions also worshiped nature and assigned meaning to many natural weather events and land formations.
5. **Arena:** drumming, songs, dances, blanket song, contributing gifts, war dance, honoring a special family, sharing gifts, dancing and singing competitions

   Crafts Fair: elders sharing stories and skills, selling handmade items, paintings and jewelry that use natural materials, playing traditional games, eating traditional foods such as fry bread

Page 82
2, 5, 1, 3, 6, 4, 7

1. reservation
2. ceremonial
3. respect
4. celebration
5. harvest

Page 88
1. Answers will vary. Possible answer: People came to honor her because she had helped so many people.
2. Their father needed help caring for the children after their mother died.
3. Arkansas, Texas, California

4. Answers will vary. Possible answer: It was a good decision because she didn't waste the molasses.
5. She had lived in Oakland for 52 years.
6. Answers will vary.

Page 89
A. 6, 10, 8, 5, 2, 4, 11, 9, 1, 7, 3
B. Sentences will vary.

Page 94
1. Tom was unhappy because he didn't know anything about his family background. He was adopted and did not know his biological parents.
2. Tom probably wanted to know about his own heritage because he was fascinated with the stories Mrs. Grill told about other Americans and their ancestors. He wanted to be able to share his heritage with the class.
3. Carlos knew about his heritage because, although he did not live with his parents, he did know who they were and had contact with them.
4. Those students in Mrs. Grill's class who didn't know about their backgrounds could bring something that symbolized a culture they admired to add to the class's melting pot.
5. The United States is sometimes called a "melting pot" because people from so many countries and cultures live there.
6. Tom said he was a melting pot because he had learned that he is made up of all the nice people he runs into each day.

Page 95
Possible answers include:
A. 1. *Biological parents* are a person's birth parents.
   2. *Adoptive parents* are the parents who adopt a person.
   3. *Tom's out* refers to a way for Tom to deal with the fact that he does not know anything about his ancestors.
   4. *Out of the picture* means "to not be a part of."
   5. *The last addition* refers to the frog in the story.
B. 1. imported
   2. cultures
   3. ancestors
   4. enthusiasm

Page 100
1. The teacher in junior high school misunderstood J. C. when he said his name and wrote "Jesse."
2. He tied the world record for the 100-yard dash at 9.4 seconds. He set the following world records: 26' 8 1/2" running broad jump, 220-yard hurdles in 22.6 seconds
3. Hitler was angry that the black athletes had won so many medals. He wanted to prove his idea that they were inferior to Germans.
4. They couldn't eat in many restaurants, live in some neighborhoods, or sit at the front of a bus.
5. The Medal of Freedom recognized Owens' achievements as an athlete and as a person who strove for success despite the obstacles of poverty and racial prejudice.

Page 101
A. 1. competed, relay
   2. sophomore
   3. discrimination
   4. befriended
   5. amateur, professional
B. 1. dictator   4. recognized
   2. successful   5. exhibitions
   3. legendary

Page 103
1. c   5. c
2. b   6. b
3. 400 meters   7. longer (2 yards longer)

Page 107
1. Danny was probably nervous when he first arrived in Chinatown because everything was new to him, and he was only a ten-year-old boy who would be spending the day with a stranger, without his father.
2. At 4:15 Danny and Cheng could be found at the Chinatown Neighborhood Center.
3. It can be assumed that Cheng's family eats a lot of seafood because it is sold at many of the markets mentioned in the story, and Cheng and Danny enjoyed seafood as part of both lunch and dinner that day.
4. Danny and Cheng seemed to enjoy their day together. At several points in the story the reader is told they smiled or laughed. At the end of the story each child expresses a desire to visit the other again sometime. Danny's

curiosity and Cheng's eagerness to share his town's art, history, and culture could also be offered as proof the boys enjoyed their day.
5. During his day in Chinatown, Danny learned some of the history of Chinatown. He learned about styles of oriental art. He learned how fortune cookies were made. He learned that some businesses operate in open-air markets. He learned the names of some Chinese food items. He learned that the Chinese are no different from people of any other culture in that they like to laugh, have fun, and even play bingo.
6. Cheng probably wants to visit Montana because spending a day showing off his own town has likely made him wonder how other towns might differ. Cheng enjoyed being Danny's tour guide so much, he wants Danny to have a turn being tour guide in his own town.

Page 108

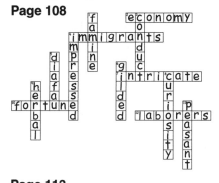

Page 113
1. b
2. A "newest-addition cousin" is a baby cousin.
3. Yes, the author did enjoy her afternoons spent on her grandparents' farm. Statements from the story that prove it are "…I adored summer Sunday afternoons," and "…I was the most reluctant to say good-bye to another Indiana Sunday."
4. The phrase means that aunts and uncles realized they needed to get home and get themselves and their children to bed so they would be able to get enough sleep to be rested for Monday morning.
5. 2, 4, 5, 1, 3, 7, 6

Page 114
1. "Then we would all be booted upstairs." *Booted* means "sent."
2. dinner–lunch
   porch–recreation room

cellar–basement
brood–family
nook and cranny–corner or small space
womenfolk–women
3. a tractor
4, 3, 1, 8, 7, 2, 5, 9, 6

Page 116
1. corn   4. HI
2. CO, WY, NV, OR   5. WI, MN, MI
3. KS, OK   6. CA, FL

Page 119
1. Possible responses may include:
Ruth Tall Chief: gave Maria the opportunity to learn piano and ballet because she felt music and dance were important, and she wanted her girls to have careers on stage; was the force behind the move to California to provide her girls with greater opportunity to perform.
Madame Nijinska: made Maria work hard and develop her talent; her influence caused Maria to decide to be a ballerina.
George Balanchine: taught Maria to use her strengths and become an even better dancer; invited her to join his company which became very popular, thus increasing Maria's popularity.
2. Possible responses may include:
Similarities: performing in front of an audience; require practicing to improve skills; much traveling to perform
Differences: Concert pianists may perform alone; ballet is most often done with other dancers. Ballet is more demanding physically. Ballet requires costumes; being a pianist does not. A pianist plays an instrument; ballet dancers perform with their bodies.
3. Possible responses may include: talented, artistic, graceful, elegant, hardworking, determined, enchanting, brilliant, electrifying, industrious, etc.

Page 120
A. Students' responses will vary.
B. 1. determined   4. retired
   2. electrifying   5. strengths
   3. original

Page 125
1. The people who gave Helen Keller money to buy a new dog were probably not upset that she wanted to use her money in a different way because she wanted to help

Celebrating Diversity • EMC 798

another child. The people who gave her the money were probably proud of Helen's kindness.

2. When Helen was a young girl, it seemed unlikely she would grow into a giving person because she herself had such severe disabilities and because she expressed so much anger before she could communicate effectively.

3. Helen Keller became known as "America's First Lady of Courage" because she did not let her disabilities stand in the way of accomplishing many things and helping many others to live full lives too.

4. Annie Sullivan was such an important part of Helen Keller's life that Helen wanted to write a book to honor her and let others know how special she was.

5. Helen traveled around the world, met many famous personalities, wrote books, and addressed countless crowds with well-received speeches and stories.

Page 126
1. count
2. wander
3. graduate
4. determine
5. frustrate
6. communicate
7. accomplish
8. organize
9. advantage
10. assist

Sentences will vary.

Page 132
1. Students' responses will vary, but should include the idea that those involved in the civil rights movement hoped to overcome or conquer the injustices being experienced by black Americans.

2. Martin probably chose to approach reform through love because the approach fit with his Christian upbringing. Also, not mentioned in the story, Martin was influenced by the work of Ghandi in India.

3. Students' responses will vary, but should be supported by clear opinion.

4. Martin was willing to go to jail because he believed it was morally correct to break unjust laws. He felt strongly enough that injustices must be corrected that he was willing to undergo personal hardships.

5. Students' responses should be supported by logic.

Page 133
1. movement
2. crusaders
3. boycott
4. abolish
5. prohibited
6. civil rights
7. discrimination
8. civil disobedience

Page 134
Facts include the following:

Determined: Continued a boycott for over a year
Continued to work for reform after buses integrated
Continued work even after being imprisoned several times

Loving: Did not resort to anger or hate when his own home was bombed
Led and encouraged peaceful demonstrations
Referred to the power of love in many speeches

Intelligent: Completed extensive schooling, earning many honors
Presented speeches that became classics of American history
Able to organize a massive movement for civil rights

Strong: Continued his mission in the face of death threats
Able to lead large groups of people
Led a movement that required both physical and mental strength

Leader: Nobel Peace Prize winner
Main organizer of and featured speaker at massive March on Washington
Organizer of countless marches, sit-ins, and kneel-ins
Became the voice of the civil rights movement

Hardworking: Printed and distributed thousands of fliers in Montgomery
Traveled extensively giving speeches
Marched countless miles

Page 137
1. General Order #3 was important because it brought word to the slaves of Galveston, Texas, that they were free.

2. Responses may include all or several of the following: The slaves of Galveston were overjoyed. They sang, talked, prayed, jumped, and shouted. Some met to discuss what they had heard, hardly believing it. Many walked or ran away from the work they had been doing. Many celebrated with song, dance, and food.

3. The first celebrations were held in Galveston and the surrounding areas.

4. The tradition spread because people moved away but brought their traditions with them, honoring Juneteenth wherever they happened to be. Others probably observed their celebrations and joined in or imitated them, pleased to honor freedom.

5. Responses may include any three of the following, or students may respond with their own Juneteenth traditions: Today people celebrate with parades, speeches, music, prayer, food, dance, plays, poetry, and sporting events. Two long-standing Juneteenth traditions are barbecue and red soda pop.

6. Students should infer that the author feels people should remember how important it is to be free. One way to remember is to honor this holiday.

Page 138
A 1. celebrating
2. celebrity
3. celebration
4. celebrants
5. celebrated

B. Students' responses will vary.

1. a special gathering or party to celebrate something
2. taking part in special activities or festivities
3. people who take part in a festivity celebrating a special occasion
4. widely known; famous
5. a person who is widely known and/or honored for a specific achievement